SPIRITS, HEROES & HUNTERS
from
NORTH AMERICAN INDIAN MYTHOLOGY

SPIRITS, HEROES & HUNTERS
from
NORTH AMERICAN INDIAN MYTHOLOGY

TEXT BY MARION WOOD
ILLUSTRATIONS BY JOHN SIBBICK

SCHOCKEN BOOKS
NEW YORK

First American edition published
by Schocken Books 1982
10 9 8 7 6 5 4 3 2 1 82 83 84 85
Copyright © 1981
by Eurobook Limited
Published by Agreement with
Eurobook Limited, London

ISBN 0-8052-3792-5

Printed and bound by
©ollins, Glasgow

THE AUTHOR
Marion Wood is Assistant Curator (Anthropology) at
the Horniman Museum in London, where there is a
small collection of North American Indian artefacts.
She is particularly interested in the art and culture of
the North American Indians and has made a special
study of Navajo weaving.

THE ARTIST
John Sibbick studied art at Guildford School of Art
and worked as a general artist in a studio for some
years. He is now a full-time freelance artist and has
specialized in accurate reconstructions of life in the
past. Chapter opening illustrations by Bill Donohoe.

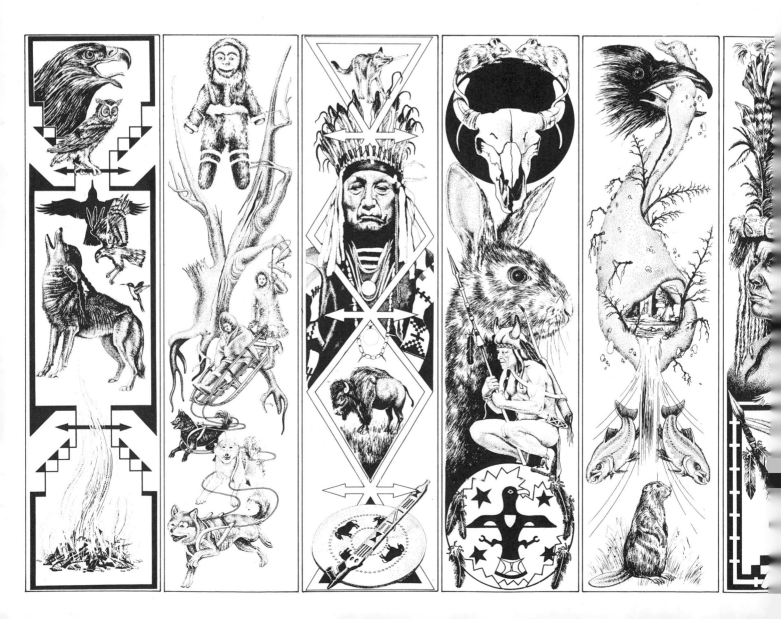

Contents

The first Americans

Archaeologists believe that the first inhabitants of America were bands of hunters who crossed the Bering Strait from Siberia about 25,000 years ago. Then much of the continent was covered with ice, but, as this began to melt, people gradually moved south until, about 10,000 years ago, they reached the very tip of South America.

With the passing of the last Ice Age, North America developed into a land of immense variety and contrast. Extending from the Arctic wastes of northern Canada and Alaska to the sub-tropical regions of Florida and California, it is a land of high mountain ranges and dense forests, fertile river valleys and wide grassy plains, swamps and deserts. The Indians of North America followed different ways of life according to the type of region which they inhabited, developing skills and traditions best suited to the natural environment and the resources which it offered.

In the far north, around the Arctic coasts, lived the Eskimos, nomadic hunters who depended on both land and sea for their livelihood. Seals, walrus, whales and caribou provided them not only with food, but also with blubber and fat for heat and light and skins for clothing, shelter and boats. In winter seals and walrus were hunted through holes cut in the ice, but in summer, when the ice broke up, they were harpooned from light canoes called kayaks. Whales were hunted from larger open boats, or umiaks, which could carry eight or ten men.

Eskimo clothing provided extremely good protection against the harsh climate. Sealskin was used for summer clothing, but warmer caribou hide was preferred for winter. Both men and women wore hooded parkas with trousers, boots and mittens, often two layers of each in very cold weather.

During the summer months people lived in skin tents, but in winter they built more permanent dwellings of stone, wood and turf. Where these materials were not available, domed snowhouses, or igloos, were constructed from blocks of hard-packed snow and ice. Several families usually lived together in one large house or in a cluster of igloos linked by a common entrance tunnel. Often, settlements consisted of only one or two such family groups, except when several groups came together for communal hunting or for religious ceremonies.

11

The coastal areas inhabited by the Eskimos were almost completely treeless, but further south stretched great forests of pine, spruce, larch and cedar. The Indians who lived here were few in number and widely scattered. They were also hunters and fishermen, travelling in small groups during the long, dark winter months and coming together in larger camps for the short summer.

Like the Eskimos, the Indians of the Northern Forests needed to consume large quantities of food in order to combat the cold and to gain energy for hunting. Caribou, moose, bears, beavers and hares were trapped or hunted with bows and arrows. Birds were caught in nets and snares, and around the lakes, fishing was important, especially at times of the year when other forms of food were scarce.

The most common shelter was a conical tent of skin or bark, which was easily constructed and transported, although in the western part of the area more substantial wooden houses were built.

Caribou and moose skins were used for making clothing and bedding, as well as bags for carrying goods and belongings. Other storage containers and dishes for cooking and serving were made from pieces of birch bark, folded into shape and then stitched with spruce roots.

Birch bark was also used for making canoes. Large sheets were fastened to a wooden framework, again with spruce roots, and the seams coated with spruce gum to make them watertight. Birchbark canoes were very light and could be easily carried around rapids or between one waterway and another.

In winter, sleds and toboggans were used for hauling goods, and snowshoes were worn, designed to prevent the wearer from sinking into the snow.

Along the rocky Pacific coast from southern Alaska to northern California the climate is much milder with a heavy rainfall, producing thick forests and heavy undergrowth. In this area the Indians had little need of warm clothing. Capes woven from shredded cedar bark and wide-brimmed basketry hats served to protect them from the rain and most of the year they went barefoot.

Wildlife was plentiful. The Indians here caught fish with hooks, nets and spears and hunted seals, sea lions and whales from canoes with harpoons. Inland, wild plants and berries were gathered and animals such as deer, bears and mountain goats were trapped or shot with bows and arrows.

Because of the wealth of readily available food, the Indians had ample leisure to develop their artistic skills, especially in woodworking. Canoes, cradles, boxes, dishes, spoons and many other items were made of wood and almost everything was elaborately carved and painted, whether it was for everyday use or, like masks and rattles, for ceremonial purposes.

Their large rectangular houses were also built of wood. Several related families, perhaps thirty or forty people, lived in each house and larger villages consisted of eight or ten houses. Each house was under the direction of a house chief with a head chief in charge of the village. Each village was independent and owned its own land, fishing grounds and hunting territory. There was no tribal chief or overall authority, although several villages might come together for ceremonies or warfare.

Each village was made up of three classes— chiefs or nobles, commoners, and slaves, who were usually war captives. There was a highly organized system of rank, based mainly on ancestry and family connections, but also related to wealth in the form of material possessions such as blankets, ceremonial copper plaques and surplus food. It was impossible to achieve high standing in society without first acquiring such wealth. To announce an important event, such as a birth or a marriage, or to establish claims of inheritance, a chief would hold a special feast called a potlatch, to which chiefs from other villages were invited. On such occasions the giver of the feast demonstrated his wealth and power by giving away, or even destroying, his possessions. In order not to be outdone by such a display of generosity, the guests had to give similar feasts in return, so that the potlatch was really an elaborate way of exchanging and distributing property.

On the other side of the country, around the Great Lakes and in the Woodlands which stretched from the Atlantic coast to the Mississippi River, the Indians also lived in large well-organized villages, often surrounded by timber stockades. Some built long rectangular houses of wood with rounded or sloping roofs of thatch or bark. Others lived in round dome-shaped huts which they called wigwams, made of bent poles covered with rush mats and sheets of bark.

Villages sometimes formed leagues for the purposes of war or trade, but there was no central government within a tribe. Although people might be linked by the same language and customs, or through ties of kinship, every village was ruled independently by an elected chief with a council to advise him and to help maintain law and order.

The Indians in this area hunted, fished and gathered wild plants like those in other areas, but they were chiefly farmers, growing many varieties of corn, beans and squash in the fields around their villages. These were the people who introduced the first European explorers and settlers to corn, potatoes and tobacco.

West of the Mississippi valley, reaching as far as the Rocky Mountains, lie the rolling prairies and grasslands known as the Great Plains. The Indians here were of many tribes, with different languages and customs, yet having much in common. All were dependent on the buffalo for food and raw materials and on the horse for transport.

Horses evolved in the New World but became extinct there long before the first Indians arrived. They were brought back by Spanish settlers in the sixteenth century, but it was not until the middle of the eighteenth century that they became common in the plains. Before then, buffalo and other game were pursued on foot. Several hunters would often join together to round up a herd and stampede it into a corral or over a cliff.

Some tribes, particularly those in the Eastern Plains, were farmers like those in the Eastern Woodlands, growing corn and other crops, but the coming of horses made hunting much easier and most tribes gave up farming to become nomadic hunters.

Those who continued to farm built houses of wood and turf, but most of the Plains Indians lived in tipis, conical tents made of poles covered with buffalo skins.

Their clothing was also made of skin, with shirts and leggings for men and long belted dresses for women. Clothing for ceremonial occasions was painted and decorated with fur, feathers and porcupine quills, although the quills were later replaced by glass beads supplied by white traders.

Every tribe was composed of several related bands, each numbering a hundred or more people. In autumn the bands separated and took to the river valleys and foothills of the Rockies to seek shelter from the cold winter winds sweeping down from the north. Here they lived in camps under the direction of a chief aided by a council of elders. With the coming of the warmer weather, they left their winter quarters and moved out into the open Plains in search of buffalo. By early summer the bands of each tribe had reunited to form a large encampment of several thousand people. At the centre of the great circle of tipis a special lodge was erected for the chiefs and their councillors to meet and plan hunting expeditions, war parties and other activities.

Warfare was a way of gaining respect and status within the tribe. Killing was not necessarily the object, for it was considered more brave and honourable to steal an enemy's horses or weapons, or to touch him and escape unscathed, than actually to kill him, and warriors vied with each other in performing daring deeds of this kind.

South-west of the Plains the landscape changes dramatically. Much of it consists of a high plateau of red and orange sandstone cut by deep canyons, with sheer-sided, flat-topped hills called mesas, and towering rocks worn into fantastic shapes by wind and rain. Forests of pine and fir cover the mountain ranges and clumps of cedar and juniper grow on the lower slopes and in the valleys, but elsewhere lies a semi-desert area, baked hard and dry by the sun and supporting only cactus and small, stunted bushes.

Nevertheless, there is enough seasonal rainfall in the South-West to make agriculture possible and the Pueblo Indians grew corn, vegetables and fruit. Pueblo, the Spanish word for a town, was applied to these Indians by the sixteenth-century Spanish explorers of this area, who were impressed by their large villages built of stone and sun-dried mud bricks. The villages consisted of several large, multi-storied houses arranged around one or more courtyards. Many buildings were terraced so that the roof of each house formed a balcony for the one above. Access to the upper stories was provided by wooden ladders which could be drawn up in time of danger.

The Pueblo Indians also grew cotton which they spun and wove into blankets and clothing. The men wore cotton shirts and kilts and the women dresses and shawls.

Each village or pueblo was governed by a chief and a council. In some cases the chief was appointed for life, but in others he was elected annually. Often a second chief was appointed to supervise the defence of the pueblo and to lead war parties.

Neighbouring tribes, like the Navajo, also grew crops, but concentrated more on hunting deer and small game. They were nomadic people and their homes were temporary shelters of brushwood in summer and of logs covered with earth in winter. Their clothing was made of skin, although they sometimes traded cotton garments from the Pueblo.

During the seventeenth century, Spanish settlers brought sheep and goats into the area and the Navajo became shepherds, moving around the country in search of water and grazing for their flocks. Later they learned to spin and weave the wool their flocks provided and to make their clothing from it.

The nomadic tribes were divided into many small bands, each with its own chief who held office for life and was often succeeded by his son if he proved worthy.

West of the Great Plains, between the Rocky Mountains and the Sierra Nevada, lies one of the most arid and inhospitable regions of North America. Today, modern irrigation has made this desert land less barren, but previously it was too dry to allow for Indian methods of cultivation.

The tribes who lived there were among the poorest in the country, but their knowledge of the land kept them from starving. The short scrubby vegetation supplied them with their main diet of seeds, roots and nuts, as well as with the materials for building their flimsy brush shelters. There were few deer to be found in this area, but the Indians made the best use of such wildlife as

there was and hunted rabbits, lizards, rats and birds. Even caterpillars and grasshoppers were not despised as food.

The search for food kept the Indians constantly on the move. For a week or so a small group would camp by a seed patch and strip it completely. Then they moved on, travelling mainly on foot.

The bulk of their clothing was made from grass and bark, but for colder weather they wove blankets from strips of rabbit fur and sometimes they managed to obtain skin clothing from the Plains tribes.

Beyond the Sierra Nevada, in what is now California, the Indians led a similarly simple existence, but here food was more abundant and life was easier. Their staple diet was a mushy porridge made from acorns pounded and boiled, and the sea provided a variety of fish and shellfish.

The richer vegetation not only made food-gathering less time consuming, but also provided the women with materials for making baskets, a craft at which they excelled. Finely woven baskets were made for all sorts of purposes. Those made as gifts or for ceremonies were especially beautiful, often decorated with clam-shell beads or covered entirely with brilliantly coloured feathers.

Just as the lives of the North American Indians differed from one area to another, so did their beliefs and myths, for these reflected their experience of the world. The hunting tribes, for example, told many stories of animal spirits, while those who were farmers were more concerned with the beings who, they believed, controlled rainfall and the growth of crops.

All these spirits had to be treated with respect and caution, for, although they could be called upon for help in time of need, they could also be dangerous and there were many complicated rules of conduct to be followed if the spirits were not to be angered and cause storms, sickness, famine and other calamities to strike mankind. Hunters, for example, often treated the animals which they killed with great ceremony so that their spirits might be placated and return to be hunted again. Those who broke the rules and offended the spirits could bring hardship and suffering not only to themselves, but to the whole community.

Many of the Indian myths explain the origin of these rules and how they should be followed.

Other stories tell of individuals receiving the help of spirits through personal contact with them. Young men wishing to make their way in the world often sought such help by going alone into remote and desolate places to fast and pray for guidance. After denying themselves food and water for several days, they often had visions in which spirits appeared to befriend them and to instruct them in rituals which would bring them wealth and success.

A man who was blessed with special help from the spirits could become a medicine man, or shaman, and use his knowledge for the good or harm of others. Shamans were believed to have powers to control the spirits and to intercede with them. In times of hardship people turned to them to find out why the spirits were displeased and how matters could be set right. The chief work of shamans lay in diagnosing and curing illness, but through their communication with the spirits they could also predict the weather, indicate where game might be found or put a curse on an enemy or evil-doer. Sometimes they accompanied war-parties to help them to victory.

Many of the myths and legends were considered sacred and could only be recounted by certain people, but others were intended purely for entertainment and could be told by anyone.

The time for telling stories was around campfires on long winter evenings, for then the Indians had leisure for such pastimes. Then too, the Indians said, the animals slept and could not be offended by overhearing the many tales which poked fun at them or showed them in a poor light.

Since the arrival of the first European settlers in the sixteenth century, much has changed for the Indians. Little of the traditional way of life remains. Guns have long since ousted bows and arrows, and motorized forms of transport have largely replaced sleds, canoes and horses. Large industrial cities now cover the old hunting grounds. Skin clothing is rarely seen except on special occasions or for the benefit of tourists. While many Indians still farm, hunt and fish in the reservations where they were placed during the nineteenth century, much of their equipment is modern and factory made. Other Indians have gone to seek employment in towns and cities far from their tribal lands.

Many ceremonies have fallen into disuse and many myths are forgotten, for they were not written down, although some were recorded in other ways — on totem poles or in sandpaintings, for example. Yet a great number are still remembered and, around winter firesides, when the animals are asleep, those with long memories continue to instruct their listeners in the customs and values of their forefathers.

The coming of Raven

The world of the Eskimos was full of spirits. The most powerful were those of the sea, the moon and the air, but there were many others, for the Eskimos believed that everything in nature — animals, mountains, lakes, even rocks and stones — had a soul or spirit which could be pleased or angered by the actions of man.

Extreme care had to be taken not to offend the souls of those animals hunted for food. Since it was believed that the sea animals disliked coming in contact with those of the land, it was forbidden to eat seal and caribou meat on the same day, or even to sew caribou-skin clothing when seal, walrus and whale were being hunted. If such rules were not observed, the animals would not allow themselves to be hunted.

Special feasts and ceremonies were held to amuse and placate the souls of dead animals. One of these was the bladder festival. The bladder of an animal was believed to contain its soul and so, when an animal was killed, the hunter carefully removed and preserved the bladder until the time came for the festival. Then, with great ceremony, the bladders were inflated and hung in a special feast-house. After much singing and dancing and offering of food, the bladders were taken down and thrust into a hole cut in the ice, so that the souls could return to the sea where they would enter the bodies of unborn animals and return again to be hunted. If these things were not done correctly, the souls of the animals would feel neglected and game would become scarce. At the beginning of the year, before the hunting season began, the Eskimos held another festival, at which animal masks were worn in order to please the animals and encourage them to return.

The ghosts of dead people could also prove harmful unless the proper procedures were followed. The dead had to be buried with everything they might need in the next world, such as clothing, food, tools and weapons. When someone died through natural causes, his soul travelled to the Narrow Land at the bottom of the sea. If he died violently, it flew up to the Land of Day in the sky towards the dawn. In these lands the ghosts lived much as they had done on earth. In the Land of Day life was especially happy and carefree and the dancing lights of the aurora borealis were said to be the souls of the dead playing their favourite game of football with a walrus skull. Regular festivals were held for the souls of the dead so that their relations could honour them with songs and dances and with offerings of food, water and clothing. If this was not done, ghosts might return to earth as evil spirits.

Many of the myths and legends told by the Eskimos are concerned with the spirits which they felt to be all around them or with natural forces which they found hard to explain. Because the Eskimos lived in small isolated groups, the stories differed from place to place. There was some disagreement, for example, about the manner in which the world had been formed. In some areas, Eskimos believed that it had always existed and that the first people came from the sky or out of the earth, but in Alaska they said that the world and everything in it was created by Raven.

In the beginning there was only darkness. Yet, in that darkness, there was already Raven. He was still small and weak and his special powers had not fully developed. In fact, he did not even know that he had special powers. He crouched in the ground in the darkness, listening. There was no sound. Nothing.

He felt around him. The ground was hard and bare. Cautiously at first, then with growing confidence, he crawled forward over the ground. Everywhere it seemed the same—hard and bare. But behind him, as he moved, things began to come to life. Water trickled out of crevices, swelling to become streams and rivers. Hills and mountains pushed up out of the earth. By the time that Raven returned to the place where he had started, he was astonished to find a forest with a thick undergrowth of grass and ferns.

Encouraged by this, he decided to explore further but, before he had gone very far, he stopped and drew back in alarm. The ground had disappeared! He was on the edge of a yawning crevasse and only empty space lay before him.

He rested under a tree and tried to puzzle it all out. Who was he? What made things grow? What lay at the bottom of the crevasse?

Perched on the edge of the chasm, he flexed his wings and felt them grow strong and powerful. All at once everything became clear. He knew who he was! He was Tulugaukuk, the Raven Father, the creator of all life. With a triumphant 'Cawk! Cawk!', he spread his wings and glided down into the silent and mysterious darkness.

Far below, he found another land, so new that the crust had barely begun to harden. Raven called this land 'earth' and the land which he had left behind he called 'sky'. Earth was barren and desolate, just as the Sky Land had been, but by his very presence Raven brought it to life and soon this land, too, was covered with trees, grass, plants and flowers.

Yet, all the while, darkness covered everything. Suddenly a pin-point of light caught his eye. Bending down, he glimpsed a fragment of mica half-hidden in the ground. As he scraped away the soil, the light grew brighter—much, much brighter. Shielding his eyes from the glare, Raven tossed the mica high in the air and in an instant the world was flooded with brilliant sunshine.

Now Raven could see what he had created. It was a wonderful land of high, snow-capped mountains, forests and wooded slopes, of grassy plains and valleys, well watered with rivers, lakes and streams, bright and shining in the clear light.

Raven walked about the beautiful new land, proudly surveying his handiwork. On the seashore a giant beach-pea vine caught his eye. It was much larger than the others, tall as a birch tree and heavy with pale green pods.

Suddenly, with a loud pop, one of the pods burst open and out tumbled a man! Startled by this unexpected apparition, Raven jumped back. The first Eskimo sat on the ground, rubbing his eyes in the bright sunlight.
'Well!' cried Raven. 'When I made that beach-pea, I never thought that something like this would come out of it!'

When they had both recovered from their surprise, Raven showed Man what he had done.
'Are you hungry?' asked Raven. 'These berries are good to eat.'

Man ate the berries, but he still felt hungry and Raven saw that something more sustaining was required. After a little thought, he took a lump of clay from the river bank and fashioned two little animals with short sturdy legs and broad, curving horns. He lowered his wings over them for a moment and, when he raised them again, two great musk-oxen bounded away over the plain.

In the same way Raven made the first pair of caribou but, because he did not allow the clay

17

long enough to dry completely before flapping his wings, the coats of the caribou remained mottled, brown and white, as they are to this day.

'I will show you how to make bows of wood and sinew,' Raven told Man, 'and arrows tipped with bone so that you can hunt these animals for meat. But take care!' he added. 'You must not hunt too many of them or they will become scarce and you will go hungry. The animals will be your friends in many ways if you treat them with respect.'

For several days Raven went about making all kinds of animals, birds and fish, and explaining their uses to Man. He told him which were best to eat and which had the finest skins. He showed him the ferocious bear so that Man would learn fear and caution. Some of the creatures which Raven made, like the tiny bright-eyed shrew and the darting water-beetle, had no practical purpose, but Raven thought that they would serve to make the world pleasant and lively.

Thinking that Man might be lonely by himself, Raven decided to give him a companion. He made a little clay figure, rather like Man in appearance, with a knot of fine grass for hair. Raven flapped his wings—and there stood the first woman!

Man learned to build his house from wood and turf, and to make skin-covered canoes, and sleds from wood and bone. He discovered how to make a fire-drill from a piece of dry wood and a strip of hide, so that fire came to warm him and cook his food. His wife made bone needles and sinew thread and learned to turn skins into warm coats and stout waterproof boots.

When their first child was born, Raven carried him to the river and rubbed clay over his body to make him grow strong and healthy. Such was Raven's power that, by the following day, the child was running about and, by the third day, he was a full-grown man.

Three more Eskimos fell from the pods of the giant beach-pea and Raven did for them all that he had done for the first. Always, he repeated his warning not to hunt too many of the animals.

The children of these men also grew very quickly, as did their children and their children's children, so that people soon became very numerous and their villages spread throughout the land. The people learned Raven's lessons well and they became bold and skilful hunters. Soon even the bear held no terrors for them. Then they grew even bolder and became greedy. They forgot Raven's warning and began to kill too many animals, far more than they needed.

Raven remonstrated with them. 'Bad times will come,' he cautioned. 'Those animals which you do not kill, you will drive away!'

The people, however, thinking that they were now stronger than Raven, paid no heed and Raven, angry and disheartened, made up his mind to leave Earth forever and return to the Sky Land. To punish the people for their wilfulness, he took the sun with him, wrapped in a caribou-skin bag.

Now darkness covered the earth again and the people became very frightened, for they could no longer see to hunt and fish. They tumbled into bogs and rivers and lost their way even in their own villages.

Now and then Raven took pity on them and uncovered the sun for a day or two to allow them to hunt a little. Then he hid it away again so that darkness and confusion reigned once more.

In the Sky Land Raven himself took a wife, a young snow goose. They had one son, Raven Boy, of whom they were very proud. Sometimes Raven would show him the sun to amuse him. The young Raven was fascinated by the bright object and longed to have it for a plaything.

One day, while Raven dozed, Raven Boy crept stealthily to the chest where the sun was stored. Carefully he lifted out the skin bag but, at that very moment, Raven awoke. In panic, Raven Boy darted to the door and, flapping his wings, soared into the darkness carrying the sun with him.

Raven rushed after him, begging him to return, but his son only flew higher and higher. Fearing that he meant to keep the sun for himself, Raven cried after him, 'Do not hide the sun forever! Let it shine on the earth sometimes.'

High in the sky, Raven Boy heard his father's words and, tearing off the skin cover, he set the sun back in its old place so that light once more returned to the earth. But it was not the unremitting light of former days, for Raven Boy feared that if the people forgot the terrors of darkness, they would forget also Raven's teaching. With a sweep of a wing, he sent the sky spinning round the earth, carrying the sun with it and in this way day and night were created.

Sedna, the witch under the sea

Sedna, the Sea Spirit, was once a mortal girl, living with her father by the seashore. She was very beautiful and many men came to court her, bringing gifts to win her favour. But Sedna was very proud and haughty and would have none of them. Always she found some fault. This one was too short or that one had bad teeth. She spurned their gifts and turned her back on them, refusing even to speak.

This behaviour infuriated her father. 'Why can you not take a husband like other girls?' he asked impatiently. 'Now that I am old, I need a son-in-law to help me with hunting.'

Sedna only shrugged carelessly and turned away, brushing her long dark hair and humming.

Finally, when yet another young man had gone away, hurt and saddened by Sedna's cruelty, her father lost his temper.
'The very next man who comes here,' he stormed, 'you shall marry! Next time I will make you! You will not refuse again!'

He did not have long to wait. The very next day a strange kayak appeared at the water's edge. In it sat a tall young man dressed in rich, dark furs. A heavy hood covered his head and his face was half-hidden by his wooden snow-goggles.

Sedna's father hurried down to the shore, dragging his struggling, protesting daughter behind him. Even before the stranger had time to disembark, the old man shouted, 'Do you seek a wife? Here is my daughter Sedna! She is young and beautiful, and can cook and sew. She will make you an excellent wife.'

The young man smiled. 'I have heard much of your daughter's beauty,' he nodded, 'and have come with the purpose of making her acquaintance.' Turning to Sedna, he went on, 'I have a large and splendid house in my own country, hung with furs to keep out the elements. If you marry me, you will sleep on soft bearskins and eat only the finest food.'

Sedna looked at the young man sitting tall and straight in his kayak. 'Well, if I must take a husband, I suppose I must,' she thought grudgingly. 'He seems kind and not too ugly. I could do worse.'

Indeed she had little choice in the matter, for her father's mind was made up and without more ado he bundled her into the kayak. The young man picked up his paddle and pushed off from the shore.

For many miles they travelled across the ice-cold sea. Sedna, cross and sulky, said nothing, nor did the young man seem inclined for conversation. Only the lapping of the water against the kayak or the occasional cry of a solitary bird disturbed the silence. On and on they went until at last a rocky island loomed out of the mists.

'Look!' said the young man. 'There is my home.'

Sedna was filled with dismay. The island seemed a bleak and inhospitable place. Nothing grew on its stony shores and seabirds swooped about the cliffs, filling the air with their wild, mournful cries.

The young man brought the kayak into the shallows and leaped ashore. He threw back his hood and pulled off his goggles. Sedna looked at him aghast. He was very ugly, short and squat, with tiny, red-rimmed eyes. He had seemed tall before only because of the high seat of his kayak. He saw Sedna's horrified face and burst into harsh, cackling laughter.

'Come!' he cried, roughly seizing her arm. 'Come and see my fine house—your new home!'

But it was not at all fine. It was nothing but a heap of twigs and driftwood perched on a high rocky ledge. There were no soft furs as the young man had promised, only a few miserable fish skins

thrown on the rough floor. Sedna looked at her new husband and, before her eyes, he turned into a small, soot-black bird. Too late she realized the truth. This was no young man whom she had married, but a storm petrel in human disguise.

Sedna regretted bitterly the foolish pride which had brought her to this terrible place. The cliff-top nest was cold and uncomfortable and there was only fish to eat, but there was no way of escape and so for a long time Sedna lived with the storm petrel on the rocky island. During the day he left the nest in his bird form and flew over the sea in search of food. When he returned in the evening he became a man once more.

Meanwhile, Sedna's father, repenting his hasty temper, decided to go in search of her and, after many days travel, he too came to the lonely rock where the storm petrel lived. When he saw his daughter's misery, he was stricken with remorse. 'Oh my poor child,' he cried, 'I did not mean you to suffer such a fate! Surely you have been punished enough! Let us return home at once.'

They climbed hastily into his kayak and set off, but, even before the island had faded from view, Sedna, looking back, saw a black speck appear. 'Father! Father!' she screamed. 'My husband is returning! When he finds me gone, he is sure to follow us. What shall we to do?'

The old man pushed her down into the bottom of the kayak and covered her over with skins. Urged on by fear, he paddled as fast as he could and the kayak flew over the waves.

Out of the darkening sky came the storm petrel, swooping low, his wings stiff and outstretched. Although Sedna was hidden under the pile of skins, he knew she was there. He flew round and round the kayak, shrieking wildly. At first the old man paid no heed, but again the bird swooped low, beating at the sea with his wings so that it grew black and angry and great waves began to wash over the kayak. The old man shouted and struck out at him with his paddle, but the bird dodged the blows and, skimming the surface of the water, beat his wings so furiously that the storm raged even more fiercely and the sea became a churning whirlpool, tossing and spinning the kayak like a child's toy, threatening to engulf it completely.

Fearing for his life, the old man lost his reason

and dragged the trembling Sedna from her hiding place. 'Here is your wife!' he cried. 'Take her for yourself,' and he hurled her into the sea.

Screaming in terror, Sedna clung to the kayak, but her father, maddened with fear, struck at her hands with his paddle, and the first joints of her fingers, frozen with cold, broke off like icicles and fell into the sea. As they bobbed away, they changed miraculously into seals, diving and twisting in the waves.

Again Sedna clung to the kayak, pleading for her life, but again her father tried to make her release her grasp, this time cutting off the second joints of her fingers. These, too, fell into the sea and became the first walrus. With her bleeding stumps, Sedna made one last despairing attempt to seize hold of the kayak, but her father had no pity and struck off the remaining joints, which took the form of whales and followed the seals and walrus down into the depths of the ocean.

Now Sedna had no more fingers and she sank to the bottom of the sea. The storm petrel circled the kayak, lamenting his lost wife. Then he turned and flew back to his bleak island home.

But Sedna was not drowned. Instead, she became the Spirit of the Sea and Mother of the Sea Beasts. Legend says that she lives still at the bottom of the sea, jealously guarding the creatures which came from her fingers. Because of her father's cruelty, she has no love for human beings. Their wicked deeds trouble her, affecting her body with sores and infesting her hair like lice. Lacking fingers, she cannot brush her hair and it becomes tangled and matted. In revenge, she calls up storms to prevent men from hunting, or keeps the sea creatures to herself.

At such times shamans must travel to the land below the sea to confess men's sins and to beg her forgiveness. Only the most powerful, who fear nothing, can undertake this journey for the way is long and dangerous, blocked by great rolling boulders, and evil spirits guard the entrance to the Sea Mother's sealskin tent. To sooth Sedna's rage and pain, the shaman must first comb her hair until it hangs clean and smooth once more. Then Sedna may feel more kindly and release the whale, walrus and seal from the great pool below her lamp, so that for a time, until they forget and sin again, people may hunt freely and without fear.

24

The origin of the winds

Long ago, when the world was still quite new, there were no winds at all, neither the gentle breeze of summer nor the fierce winter gale. Everything was perfectly still. Nothing disturbed the marsh grass on the shore and, when snow fell, it fell straight to earth instead of blowing and swirling into drifts as it does now.

At that time, in a village near the mouth of the Yukon River, there lived a couple who had no children. This made them very sad. Often the woman would sigh and say, 'How happy we would be if only we had a child!'

Her husband would sigh too and answer, 'Yes, if we had a son, I would teach him to stalk bears and seals over the ice-floes, and to make traps and snares. What will become of us in our old age with no one to provide for us? Who will give festivals for our souls when we are dead?'

These thoughts troubled them deeply and on many a long winter evening they sat in the flickering firelight, imagining how different life might be if they had a child.

One night the woman had a strange dream, in which she saw a sled pulled by three dogs, one brown, one white and one black, draw up outside her door. The driver leaned from his seat and beckoned her. 'Come,' he said. 'Sit here by me. I will take you on a journey.'

Wondering and fearful, the woman did as she was told. No sooner had she seated herself than the driver cracked his whip and the sled rose high into the air. Through the night-black sky they flew, faster and faster, past stars sparkling like hoar-frost. The woman was no longer afraid for she knew that this must be Igaluk, the Moon Spirit, who often comes to comfort those in distress.

Suddenly the sled stopped and the panting dogs lay down to rest. On all sides, as far as the eye could see, lay a great plain of smooth ice, the glittering expanse broken only by one small stunted tree.

Igaluk pointed and said, 'You who so desire a child, look at that tree over there. Make a doll from its trunk and you will find happiness.'

Before she could learn more, the woman awoke. So vivid was her dream that she at once roused her husband. She told him what she had seen and begged him to find the tree.

The man rubbed the sleep from his eyes. 'What would be the point?'

he grumbled. 'It would only be a doll, not a real child.' But the woman persisted and finally, for the sake of peace, the man shouldered his axe and set out to look for the tree.

At the edge of the village where the snow lay thick and untrodden, he saw a bright path stretching far into the distance. It was now full day, yet the path shone like moonlight and the man knew that this was the direction which he must take.

For many hours he journeyed along the path of light until at last, on the horizon, he saw something shining very brightly. As he came nearer he saw that it was the tree of which his wife had spoken. The man cut it down with his axe and carried it home.

That evening, while he carved the figure of a small boy from some of the wood, his wife made a little suit of sealskin and, when the doll was finished, she dressed it and set it in the place of honour on the bench opposite the door. From the remaining wood the man carved a set of toy dishes

and some tiny weapons, a spear and a knife, tipped with bone. His wife filled the dishes with food and water and set them before the doll.

Before going to bed, the couple sat and gazed at the doll. Although it was no more than six inches high, it was very lifelike, with eyes made from tiny chips of ivory.

'I cannot think why we have gone to all this trouble,' said the man gloomily. 'We are no better off than before.'

'Perhaps not,' replied his wife, 'but at least it will give us amusement and something to talk about.'

During the night the woman awoke suddenly. Close at hand she heard several low whistles. She shook her husband and said, 'Did you hear that? It was the doll!'

They jumped up and, by the glow of their hastily lit lamp, they saw that the doll had eaten the food and drunk the water. They saw it breathe and its eyes move. The woman picked it up in her arms and hugged it.

They played with the doll for some time until it grew sleepy. Then they carefully returned it to the bench and went back to bed, delighted with their new toy.

In the morning, however, when they awoke, the doll had gone. Rushing outside, they saw its footprints leading away through the village. They followed as fast as they could, but at the edge of the village the tracks stopped and there was no trace of the doll. Sadly the couple returned home.

Although they did not know it, the doll was travelling along the path of light which the man had taken the day before. On and on he went until he came to the eastern edge of day where the sky comes down to meet the earth and walls in the light.

Looking up, the doll saw a hole in the sky wall, covered over with a piece of skin. The cover was bulging inwards, as if there was some powerful force on the other side. The doll was curious and, drawing his knife, he slashed the cords holding the cover in place and pulled it aside.

At once a great wind rushed in, carrying birds and animals with it. The doll peered through the hole and saw the Sky Land on the other side, looking just like earth, with mountains, trees and rivers.

When he felt that the wind had blown long

enough, the doll drew the skin cover back over the hole, saying sternly, 'Wind, sometimes blow hard, sometimes soft, and sometimes not at all.' Then he went on his way.

When he came to the south, he saw another piece of skin covering an opening in the sky wall and bulging as before. Again the doll drew his knife and this time a warmer wind blew in, bringing more animals, trees and bushes. After a time the doll closed up the opening with the same words as before and passed on towards the west.

There he found yet another opening like the others, but this time, as soon as the cords were cut, the wind blew in a heavy rainstorm with waves and spray from the great ocean on the other side. The doll hastened to cover up the hole and instructed this wind as he had done the others.

When he came to the north, the cold was so intense that he hesitated for some time before he dared to open the hole in the sky there. When he finally did so, a fierce blast whistled in, with great masses of snow and ice, so that the doll was at once frozen to the marrow and he closed that opening very quickly indeed.

Admonishing the wind as before, the doll now turned his steps inwards, away from the sky wall, and travelled on until he came to the very centre of the earth's plain. There he saw the sky arching overhead like a huge tent, supported on a framework of tall slender poles. Satisfied that he had now travelled the whole world over, the doll decided to return to the village from which he had started.

His foster-parents greeted him with great joy, for they feared that he had gone forever. The doll told them and all the people of the village about his travels and how he had let the winds into the world. Everyone was very pleased for with the winds came good hunting. The winds brought the birds of the air and the land animals, and they stirred up the sea currents so that seals and walrus could be found all along the coast.

Because he had brought good fortune as the Moon Spirit had predicted, the doll was honoured in special festivals ever afterwards. Shamans made dolls like him to help them in their magic and parents also made dolls for their children, knowing that they bring happiness to those who care for them.

The woman and the giant

Eskimos often explain strange stories by saying that they were first told in the days when unbelievable things could happen. Then, fabulous monsters inhabited the world, like the amikuk, a great slimy sea-serpent, and the aziwugum, an animal resembling a dog, but with a black scaly body and a tail so powerful that a single blow from it could kill. There was the fierce palraujuk, a strange dragon-like creature, and a whole family of grotesque half-human beings called the kukilaluit who, with their long, razor-sharp claws, tore to pieces anyone unlucky enough to cross their path.

Fortunately, there were other less malevolent beings, such as the shadow people who were completely invisible to the human eye; only their shadows on the ground betrayed their presence. In the mountains lived mischievous dwarfs, who lay in wait to trip up unwary travellers. Their victims rarely caught a glimpse of them, for they were extremely swift-footed and could outrun any animal.

The far north was inhabited by a race of giants, so tall that their heads were hidden in the clouds. They crossed wide rivers and mountain ranges in a single stride and, when they hunted, they slung bears and caribou from their belts as ordinary men might carry mice. Yet, in spite of their great size, they were generally harmless and often kind and helpful to those in need.

Once, a woman travelling alone across the snow-covered tundra unwittingly encountered such a giant. She had fled several days before from her cruel husband, whose evil temper had made him hated and feared by everyone in the village where they lived. The slightest thing enraged him and he fought constantly with his neighbours. Children hid in terror at his approach and even his own dogs snarled when they heard his footsteps.

To his wife he was especially brutal, ceaselessly abusing and tormenting her and often beating her cruelly. At last she could endure no more and one snowy winter night, while her husband slept, she packed a small basket with food, drew on her boots and mittens, and crept quietly out of the house. Her heart pounded for she knew that if the dogs barked and roused her husband, he would beat her as never before. To her relief, nothing stirred in the village and soon she had left it far behind.

All that night and for several days afterwards she walked through the snow without meeting another human being. She avoided any villages she saw in the distance, fearing to trust strangers who might force her to return home. As she travelled, the wind grew keener and the cold more severe. Her little stock of food was soon exhausted and she was reduced to eating handfuls of snow to assuage her hunger.

Just as she was about to collapse from cold and hunger, she stumbled by chance upon a heap of freshly killed caribou, half-hidden under the snow. She could scarcely believe her good fortune! Clearly it was a cache left by some hunters who planned to return at a later date to claim their spoil. The woman looked about, but there was no one in sight.
'There is so much food here,' she thought, 'that I am sure no one would mind if I helped myself to just a little.' Hastily gathering a few sticks, she built a fire in the shelter of a nearby hill and roasted some of the meat.

When she had eaten her fill and rested, she felt much stronger and so, having filled her basket with the remainder of the cooked meat, she set off up the hill.

It really was a most curious shape, that hill, rather like a human foot, with five hummocks ranged along its summit. By the time the woman reached the top, darkness was beginning to fall and she decided to stop for the night. She brushed away the snow from between two of the hummocks and settled down. It was surprisingly warm and comfortable and the woman slept soundly until morning.

For the next three days she continued travelling along a gentle slope leading northwards. Each night she managed to find a comfortable place to stop. On the first night she sheltered under a low mound and, on the second, she snuggled cosily into a deep hollow in the ground. Towards evening on the third day, she found herself deep in a thick, dark forest. The undergrowth was dense and tangled, but it provided a warm bed and again she slept well.

Next morning, just as she was about to start off again, a gruff voice boomed from somewhere overhead, 'Who are you? What has brought you here to me, to whom human beings never come?'

Stricken with terror, the woman realized that for the last few days she had been making her way along the body of a sleeping giant, resting first between his toes, next under his knee, then in his navel and now — among his beard! It must have been the giant's caribou which she had cooked and eaten on that first night!

Although almost fainting with fright, the woman managed to stammer out her story. The deep voice spoke again. 'You may stay here if you wish, but you must never again sleep so close to my mouth, for, if I were to breathe on you, you would be blown far away.'

The woman saw that the giant meant her no harm and her fear abated.
'You must be hungry after your long journey,' continued the giant. 'Wait here and I will bring you something to eat.' The sky darkened suddenly and the woman saw a great dark cloud coming towards her. She drew back trembling, but it was only the giant's hand which opened and dropped some caribou meat at her feet. 'You may build a fire from my beard,' he said kindly. 'I shall not miss a few grey hairs.'

When the woman had finished eating, the giant said apologetically, 'I am afraid that some frost has gathered in my lungs overnight and I must cough to clear it. Go down into the thickest part of my beard and hold on tightly. Quickly now, I cannot wait any longer.'

The woman had barely time to obey before she heard a tremendous rumbling and a furious gale rushed overhead, carrying with it a blinding snowstorm.
'Ah, that's better!' said the giant and the sky became clear once more.

Soon the two became good friends. The giant, whose name was Kinak, allowed the woman to live by the side of his nose, well out of range of his mouth, and to build a hut out of hairs taken from his beard.

He provided plenty of food for both of them merely by stretching out a hand and catching caribou or deer or seals or whatever was wanted. He also caught bears, wolves and foxes, so that the woman could make warm clothing for herself and soon she had a handsome store of skins and furs.

Thus they lived amicably for some time. Now

and again the woman could not help thinking of her husband and wondering whether he missed her and was sorry for having driven her away.

Kinak noticed that sometimes she looked sad and thoughtful, and one day he asked her if she would like to return home.

'Yes, I would,' admitted the woman, 'but I am so afraid that my husband will beat me again.'

'Never fear,' Kinak replied. 'I will protect you. If ever you are in danger, you have only to call my name and I will save you.'

Kinak told the woman to cut the ear tips off all the skins which she had stored and to put the tips in her basket. When she had done so, he told her to crouch down by his lips and to close her eyes.

All at once there came a great blast of wind and snow and the woman felt herself lifted and driven through the air before it, carried like a feather on Kinak's breath.

At last, when the wind dropped and her feet touched solid ground once more, she opened her eyes. She was back in her village, standing before her old home. She put the basket of ear tips in the storeroom and went into the house.

Her husband was sitting by the fire and he jumped up in alarm, thinking her a ghost, for he had long since given her up for dead. When he heard her story, he welcomed her back with joy, promising never to treat her badly again.

Next morning, when he went to the storeroom, he was astonished to find it full of rich furs, for every ear tip had turned into a complete pelt during the night. These skins made him very wealthy and he became a man of importance in the village.

For several years he kept his promise to his wife and they were very happy. A son was born to them and they called him Kinak in memory of the giant.

In time, however, the man returned to his old ways and began to treat his wife harshly once more. One day, in a fit of temper over some trifling matter, he seized a club and threatened to beat her. The woman fled out of the house, but her husband followed her and, knocking her to the ground, raised his arm to strike again.

The woman had almost forgotten the giant, but in that instant she thought of him and she cried out, 'Kinak! Kinak! Help me!'

Scarcely had she spoken when the sky grew dark and a furious whirlwind swept down upon them. The man was lifted high in the air and blown further and further away, until at last he was out of sight. Gradually the wind died away and all became still, but the cruel husband was never seen again.

The woman continued to live in the village with her son Kinak, who grew up to be a handsome young man, tall and strong. Alas, much to his mother's sorrow and dismay, he had inherited his father's evil temper and was constantly involved in brawls and disputes. One day he quarrelled with two hunting companions over a seal and killed them both with his spear.

His mother was horrified when she heard of the terrible deed. 'Your wickedness has brought shame and disgrace upon the whole village,' she told him. 'Now you have put us in great danger, for the families of those you have murdered will come here seeking revenge. It would be better for everyone if you left here and did not come back.'

So Kinak went away from the village, never to return. By chance he took the same road as his mother had done all those years before and in time he came to the land where the giant lived.

The giant was pleased to welcome the son of his old friend. He allowed the young man to live on his face and to build a hut from his beard as his mother had once done. He also repeated his old warning that, if young Kinak valued his safety, he should not come too close to his mouth.

But the young man was headstrong and scorned danger, and he made up his mind to explore the forbidden place. He pushed his way through the wiry, tangled thicket of the giant's beard and emerged close to his mouth.

At that moment the giant's lips parted and a gust of wind burst from them. The young man tried vainly to cling to the giant's moustache, but the force of the gale tore him free and hurled him far into the sky, where he disappeared into the clouds forever.

Since that day the giant Kinak has not been seen, nor has anyone dared to seek him out. It is said that he still lives in the far north and on wild winter nights his breath can be heard whistling among the drifting snow.

Hare and Otter

The Indians of the Northern Forests, hunting alone or in small groups among the the tall, dark pine trees, did not find it hard to believe themselves surrounded by supernatural beings. Kutchin and Tanaina hunters, for example, feared that a strange whistling noise heard in the woods betrayed the presence of the Nakani, evil spirits who looked like men, but who possessed superhuman powers. The Nakani abducted people, killing them or making them their slaves, and few of those they captured ever returned to tell the tale. Those who did manage to escape were strangely afflicted, driven mad by the horrors of their captivity.

The Indians tried in many ways to appease the spirits which affected their daily lives, such as those of wind and snow, of the animals which they hunted, and of the woods, lakes and rivers which formed their environment. Most people carried amulets to protect them and bring good fortune, perhaps a stone or a small animal skin, but it was the shamans who knew best how to control the spirits and it was they who usually interceded on behalf of others.

Most shamans received their special knowledge in dreams, sometimes in early childhood. This gave them the power to summon animal spirits to direct them when they were required to work their magic, and often they were believed to speak through animals or take their forms. Their equipment included amulets representing the spirits which they controlled, the skins of their spirit helpers and special cups and spoons used in healing ceremonies.

There were a number of practices relating to the killing of animals and the disposal of the bones and uneaten portions. In the James Bay area the first goose killed each spring was of particular importance and its head, dried and decorated with beads, was kept in a special place in honour of the goose spirit. Similar rituals were attached to the killing of wolves, wolverines and lynx in other areas, but the most important game animal of all was the bear. When a hunter found a bear, he spoke to it respectfully, asking permission to take its life, and explaining that only his need for food made the deed necessary. After the bear had been killed, its body was carried back to the camp with great ceremony and a feast held in its honour. The bones were placed on a special rack and the skull, sometimes painted and decorated, was tied to a tree facing a lake or stream, since this was thought to be pleasing to the spirit of the bear.

Over this vast track of forest land, the myths and legends varied considerably. In the western part of the area there were many stories concerning Raven, similar to those told by the Eskimos. Here too, the Indians told how Raven brought the sun and filled the waters with fish.

Further east, along the shores of the Great Lakes, many of the tribes spoke with awe and reverence of the great spirit, Gitche Manitou, a mysterious force which permeated everything in nature. Although Gitche Manitou was generally regarded as the creator of life and as a source of good, he took no visible form and never appeared in any of the myths.

On the other hand, many stories are told of the being who came later, often after the world was already inhabited, to mould it into its present form. This being appears under different names, according to the various tribes. Some call him Gluskap, others Michabo, Nanabozho or Wisagatcak, but the stories show that, whichever name he is given, he is usually that two-sided character so common in North American mythology, the trickster-creator. Often he appears as a wise and noble benefactor, performing useful deeds for the benefit of his fellows. At other times, he is revealed as a complete villain, crafty, malicious and deceitful.

Sometimes he is known simply as the Great Hare, for he often assumes the appearance of a hare. It was in this form, for instance, that he stole fire from the Dawn People. When the Dawn Man and his daughters found a small shivering hare in the snow outside their door, they took pity on him and brought him into the warmth of their fire. As soon as their backs were turned, however, Hare seized a burning log from the fire and ran swiftly to where he had hidden his canoe. He paddled so fast that the breeze he created caused the fire to blaze up and singe his ears. As a result of this, whatever colour the hare's coat turns, whether brown in summer or white in winter, the tips of his ears always remain dark.

Yet, in spite of his cunning, Hare is also foolish and gullible, and many of his schemes land him in a good deal of trouble.

One cold winter's day Hare was loping dejectedly through the snowy forest. He had left home early that morning in search of food, but so far had found nothing.

In a clearing near a river he came across a solitary birchbark wigwam and approached it optimistically, hoping that the occupants might prove hospitable to a weary traveller. As he drew near, Otter emerged, carrying on one shoulder a stout pole from which dangled a number of hooks.

'Greetings, brother Otter!' said Hare mournfully. 'This is a hard time of year, is it not? I haven't eaten for days and I am sure that my ribs are about to burst through my skin.' He patted his white furry sides to prove his point.

Otter laughed. 'It isn't so bad for all of us,' he said complacently. 'There is always food to be found if you know how. Come with me. I'll show you how I manage.'

Hare, scenting a meal in the offing, needed no second invitation and he followed Otter down to the river bank. From the top of the bank a smooth path of ice led down to the water's edge. Otter seated himself at the top of this path and slid smoothly down its length, plunging into the river with scarcely a ripple. He glided effortlessly about in the water, now and then ducking below the surface, and in no time at all he emerged, clutching an armful of fat, juicy eels.

Hare was full of admiration as he watched Otter hook his catch on to his pole. 'Well!' he said to himself. 'If that isn't an easy way of getting a living!'

To Hare's delight, Otter invited him to share his meal and they returned to the wigwam carrying the pole between them, for it now weighed heavily under the load of eels.

Otter's wife already had a cooking pot bubbling on the fire and soon a savoury eel stew was prepared. Hare ate heartily until he could eat no more. At last he leaned back with a satisfied sigh.

'How well some people manage to live!' he thought, wiping gravy from his whiskers. 'If Otter can do it, why can't I? I am sure that I can catch eels as well as he can.' And in anticipation of the bounty that was soon to be his, Hare graciously invited Otter to be his guest on the following evening.

On his return home, Hare found his grandmother, with whom he lived, impatiently awaiting his arrival, for there was no food of any kind in the house. When she saw that he had brought nothing, but had evidently eaten very well himself, she was extremely annoyed and said so in no uncertain terms.

'Do not fret, Grandmother,' said Hare soothingly. 'Tomorrow we are going to have a splendid feast and I have invited Otter to share it with us.'

'That's all very well!' retorted the old woman angrily. 'But where is the food to come from, may I ask? We have nothing at all and you do not seem to be much of a hunter!'

'Aha!' said Hare smugly. 'Just you wait and see what I have in mind,' and he refused to be drawn any further on the subject.

Next day Hare set about his preparations. First he cut down a small sapling. Then he made a number of hooks out of pieces of bone and lashed them to the sapling with strips of hide.

His grandmother watched in utter perplexity, wondering what he could possibly be up to.

Finally, when everything was ready, Hare said to her, 'Now then, Grandmother, fill your pot with water and set it on the fire. There will soon be lots of cooking to do.'

The old woman was still very sceptical about the promised feast, but nevertheless she did as he asked. Then she followed him down to the river to see what would happen next.

Using a birchbark dish which he had borrowed from his grandmother, Hare scooped up water from the river and poured it carefully down the bank. The weather was so cold that the water froze almost immediately, turning into a thick sheet of ice. Hare clambered to the top of the bank and pushed himself down the ice as he had seen Otter do.

However, the ice was not as smooth and slippery as Otter's well-worn ice-run had been, and Hare's descent was anything but graceful. He bumped and slithered down the slope in ungainly fits and starts and finally tumbled into the water with a tremendous splash.

The iciness of the water quite took his breath away. It filled his eyes and ears and, when he tried to gasp for air, it filled his mouth as well. He plunged about, struggling to keep his head above water, completely out of his element.

Just at that moment Otter appeared. The strange scene which met his eyes filled him with mystification.

'Isn't that your grandson in the river?' he asked the old woman. 'What *is* he trying to do?'

'I think he is fishing,' said Hare's grandmother wryly. 'I expect that he has seen someone else do this and thinks that he can do it too.'

'Hey! Come out of there!' shouted Otter in exasperation. 'Let me do that for you!'

Hare crawled out of the water, half-drowned and shivering with cold. Otter dived in and soon returned with a plentiful supply of eels. He hooked the eels on to the pole which Hare had prepared and silently passed it to him.

'I expect that I shall master the technique soon,' said Hare sheepishly, his teeth chattering with cold. 'I just need a little more practice.'

'I wouldn't bother if I were you,' replied Otter scornfully. 'You are clearly not suited to this line of work.'

Hare's grandmother, fearing that a quarrel was about to break out, intervened hastily. 'We certainly have a lot to thank you for, Otter,' she said. 'Such an abundance of eels! I hope that you will join us for supper.'

Otter shook his head. 'No, thank you,' he answered. 'Hare's ridiculous exhibition has made me quite lose my appetite,' and he strode away into the forest.

That evening, a delicious aroma wafted from Hare's wigwam as his grandmother cooked the eels, but Hare was so mortified by his abject failure as a fisherman and by Otter's withering comments that he could scarcely bring himself to eat one mouthful of the tasty dish which she set before him.

For several days he continued to brood on the incident and at last he made up his mind to seek revenge on Otter.

Hare approached Otter's wigwam with great

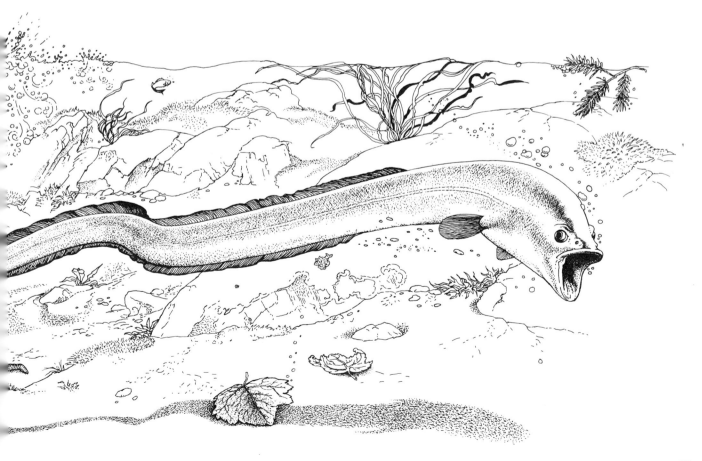

stealth, dodging from tree to tree. Neither Otter nor his wife were in sight. Hare tiptoed up to the wigwam and peered inside. It was empty but, hanging from a hook, was a string of freshly caught eels. Hare seized the eels and darted back into the shadows of the forest.

When Otter returned, he noticed at once that the string of eels was missing. He also spotted Hare's footprints in the snow and knew who the culprit was. Muttering furious threats, he set off in pursuit.

Hare knew that Otter would not find it difficult to follow his tracks and so he decided to resort to disguise. One of Hare's most useful qualities was his ability to change into anything he wished and he now turned himself into a wrinkled old woman sitting in a wigwam. No sooner had he done so than Otter appeared in the doorway.

Otter was dumbfounded to find a little old woman sitting beside her fire, for he had followed Hare's trail this far and had expected to corner him there.

'Have you seen a hare with a string of eels?' he asked. 'His tracks lead right to your door.'

'Hare?' quavered the old woman. 'Hare? What is that?'

'A little white creature,' explained Otter, 'very ugly, with long ears and not much tail.'

'I don't think that I have seen such an animal,' replied the old woman. 'I am afraid that I cannot help you, but, now that you are here, perhaps you would do me a favour? I am very cold and my fire is low. Could you possibly gather me some kindling?'

Otter was impatient to be on his way, but he felt that he could hardly refuse the old woman's pitiful request, so he set off to collect firewood.

When he returned, he was bewildered to find no trace either of the wigwam or of the old woman. Where she had sat, however, he saw the imprints of Hare's paws. Otter continued on his way, more than ever determined to catch his enemy and relieve him of the eels.

Soon he came to another wigwam. A young man was standing by the door, polishing a club of caribou antler.

'Has a hare passed this way?' asked Otter.

With a puzzled frown, the man replied, 'Do you mean a rather handsome animal with silky white fur and long legs? Could that be him behind that tree over there?'

Otter turned to look and at once received a stunning blow on the head which knocked him to the ground. When he recovered, the young man and his wigwam had vanished and he knew that he had been tricked once more.

Meanwhile Hare was running through the forest, trailing the string of eels behind him. He knew that he could not hope to keep up his series of disguises forever. Sooner or later, Otter was bound to challenge him and he was not sure what to do next.

Through the trees ahead he glimpsed a lake with a solitary fisherman in a birchbark canoe floating peacefully on its surface. Hare began to have the glimmering of an idea and he hid behind a tree.

Otter came charging out of the woods and down to the water's edge. As Hare had thought might happen, Otter took the fisherman for yet another of Hare's cunning disguises. Shouting angrily, he plunged into the lake and struck out strongly towards the canoe.

The fisherman saw what appeared to be a ferocious monster swimming towards him, with bared teeth and glittering eyes, and, having his fish spear to hand, he quickly hurled it in Otter's direction.

Luckily for Otter, the spear flew wide, but it was enough to make him stop suddenly and tread water. He saw the fisherman take up his bow and pull an arrow from his quiver and he realized to his horror that he had made a terrible mistake. He waited to see no more, but dived under the water and made swiftly for the bank. Once safely round a bend in the lake, he climbed out to rest and recover from his fright. He decided that he had had enough excitement for one day and that he would pursue Hare no longer, even if it did mean losing his eels. As he returned home, he vowed that he would have nothing more to do with Hare ever again.

Hare, too, made his way homeward. He was really looking forward to his supper of eels this time, but he wondered if he ought perhaps to concentrate on food more easily obtainable in future. On the other hand, eels were so delicious and if he practised on his ice-run. . . .

The seven sisters

The stars were important to the Indians. It was from the stars that they took their directions when they travelled at night and it was by their movements that they judged the changing of the seasons. The cluster of stars called the Pleiades particularly caught their imagination and they told many stories of how they came to be. Some said that they were a group of boys who danced so fast that they swirled up into the sky and remained there, dancing forever. Others claimed that they were six hunters and their dog, who broke the hunting rules and were taken to the sky as a punishment. Yet others believed them to be seven beautiful sisters, the daughters of the sun and moon.

One evening in summer a young man went fishing in a lake near his village. The last rays of the sun, slanting through the tall pine trees, caught the glittering waves as they broke gently on the sandy shore. Birds soared overhead or bobbed lazily on the waters. Everything was very peaceful.

Just as he was about to push his birchbark canoe out onto the lake, the young man thought that he heard the strains of distant singing. He stood still and looked about, but there was no one in sight. The singing came closer, a strange unearthly sound. It seemed to come from high above him. The young man looked up, shielding his eyes from the dying sun, and saw a large basket descending through the sky. He drew back into the shadow of the trees and waited.

The basket came to rest on the nearby shore and from it stepped seven young girls, tall and slender, dressed in purest white. Still singing, they linked hands and began to dance on the sand.

Slow and stately they danced, with light and graceful movements, their long dark hair floating about their shoulders. Their song rose up, clear and sweet, into the still evening air. The young man thought that he had never seen or heard anything so lovely as those maidens as they danced and sang in the twilight. So utterly bewitched was he by the scene before him that, before he could stop himself, he burst out singing too.

The singing ceased abruptly. The girls ran like startled deer towards their basket and climbed in. Before the young man could reach the spot, the basket had risen into the air and vanished among the clouds.

Throughout the following day, the young man thought of what he had seen. In his mind's eye he saw the girls dancing on the shore and the sounds of their music rang in his ears. That evening, as the sun began to set, he hurried down to the lake, hoping that they might come again.

He was not disappointed, for he had barely had time to conceal himself behind a large rock before he heard the singing, faint at first, then coming nearer and nearer, until at last the basket landed on the shore.

Once again the girls sang and danced before him. On this evening they danced singly, one at a time. Each appeared more beautiful than the one before and the last was the loveliest of all. The young man watched her, scarcely daring to breathe for fear he should break the spell. Wishing for a better view, he stole closer, but his eager haste made him careless and his foot dislodged a pebble, sending it clattering down the bank. In an instant the dancers fled and the basket rose and disappeared into the sky as before.

The young man returned home, sick at heart. Would they come again? Would he ever see again the lovely maiden who had so entranced him? All through the next day he thought of her constantly and he made up his mind that, should the chance present itself, he would capture her and keep her for his own.

He could scarcely wait for evening and, long before the sun had begun his downward journey, he set himself to wait by the lake.

The hours passed interminably. The young man strained his ears for the sweet singing which heralded the approach of the maidens, but time and time again his hopes were dashed, for it was only the cry of a bird or the waves lapping at the water's edge. The sun was sinking fast and he began to despair. Perhaps he had frightened them away forever. Perhaps they would never come again.

At last he heard it, the music for which he had waited so long and so impatiently. He started up eagerly and this time his senses did not deceive him. The basket was descending once more from the sky.

The girls climbed out of the basket and stood still for a moment, huddled together, looking timorously along the shore of the lake.

The young man heard one say, 'Is it safe, do you think? I cannot forget that voice which joined in our singing.'

'It was only the wind in the trees,' said another soothingly, 'nothing more.'

'But what of the noise which disturbed us last night?' asked the first nervously. 'Surely there was something lurking among those rocks?'

'An animal or a bird, perhaps,' returned the other. 'Do not worry. There is nothing to fear. No one knows that we dance here in the evenings. Come, it grows late. Soon the sun will set and we must return home. Let us begin our dance.'

So, their fears allayed, the girls circled and glided once more on the beach and their voices, raised in song, floated over the peaceful waters of the lake.

The young man inched his way slowly and carefully towards them, keeping in the shadow of the rocks and bushes until he was very close. He was more than ever determined to catch the girl with whom he had fallen in love. He waited until she was furthest away from the basket, then he sprang forward and seized her by the arm.

Screaming in terror, the other girls scattered. They rushed to the basket and tumbled into it. They called to their captured companion, their voices shrill with panic, and held out their arms to her. The girl broke free and ran to the basket, but, just as she seized hold of the edge, the young man caught her again and held her tightly in his arms.

The basket was already swinging in mid-air. The girl's fingers slipped from the rim and both she and her captor fell to the ground. The anguished cries of the occupants faded as the basket rose higher and higher. Soon it was no more than a distant speck against the sky. Then it was gone.

The young man and the girl rose to their feet and looked warily at one another. The girl said angrily, 'What do you mean by this? Why have you torn me from my sisters?'

The young man told her how he had fallen in love with her as he watched her dancing and he pleaded with her to remain with him and be his wife. The girl's gaze softened as he poured out his love for her.

'I cannot remain on earth,' she answered sorrowfully, 'though nothing would please me more. My sisters and I are the daughters of Sun

and Moon. We are the Pleiades, that group of stars which you may have seen in the sky. That is my home and I must return there.'
'Then let me come with you!' cried the young man. 'I cannot let you go!'
'That is not so easy,' replied the girl. 'I fear that my father would not welcome you. He has forbidden us to dance here and that is why we come only when he is low in the sky and cannot see us. He would be angry if he knew that we had disobeyed him.'
'Let me speak with him,' urged the young man. 'Perhaps I can persuade him to let us remain together.'
The girl thought the matter hopeless, but, touched by the sincerity of the young man's feelings and by those which she already had for him, she at last agreed.
'Well,' she sighed, 'we can at least try. I will send a message on the wind to my sisters, asking them to

let down the basket once more, so that we may both return to the sky.'
The next evening, in answer to her message, the basket came down by the lake. The six girls in it looked at the young man fearfully, but their sister explained that he was to be her husband and would return with them. They climbed into the basket and were carried up into the Sky Land.
Sun was indeed furious when he learned of his daughters' defiance of his wishes. 'Why can you not be content with your own home?' he shouted. 'Is the earth so much more beautiful that you prefer to dance and play there?'
The girls hung their heads and wept, but the young man pleaded so eloquently in their favour that Sun's heart was moved and finally he said, 'I see that you truly love my daughter, so I will allow you to remain here. But I will banish you all to the furthest part of the heavens so that you can never again visit the earth!'

'May we not go there sometimes?' asked the young man coaxingly. 'We would always return.'

The girls gasped at the young man's boldness and Sun scowled. Then he relented. 'Very well,' he replied grudgingly. 'You and your wife may return, now and then, for a short time only. But as for you others,' he cried, rounding on his remaining daughters, 'you must never go there again! One husband from the earth is quite enough!'

Sun placed the seven sisters so far away in the Sky Land that their bright and shining faces can barely be seen. Now and again, the young man and his wife visit the earth for a time and that is why, sometimes, only six stars can be seen among the Pleiades.

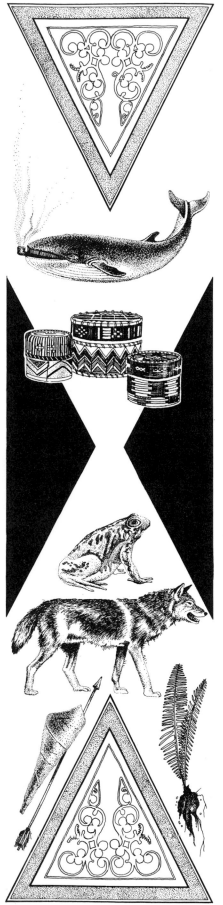

Gluscap, Lord of the North

Many stories are told by the Micmac Indians of their legendary hero Gluskap. Little is known of his origins, only that he came to the shores of the newly formed world in a great stone canoe, which later turned into an island still to be seen off the coast of Nova Scotia. Gluskap's bow was also made of stone and only he had the strength to pull it. He shot his arrows into the trees and from the bark the first people emerged.

The animals which already existed were large and powerful. The moose was of such immense size that it towered above the forests, browsing on the tops of trees. Gluskap made a whistle of birchbark and called the animal to him. He seized it in an iron grasp, squeezing and compressing it until it became the size it is now. Since then hunters have always used birchbark whistles to call the moose. The beavers, too, were strong and fierce. Gluskap found that they had taken all the water in the country for themselves, but he broke down their huge dam and released the water, creating lakes and rivers for everyone to use.

In those early days the world was cold and desolate, but Gluskap drove away the giants of ice and snow, so that they dared to trouble the world only when he slept. He pulled down the great birds which hid the sun and pinioned the wings of those which caused gales and storms, releasing them only when wind was needed. The world was a better place for Gluskap's coming.

Yet in everything he did, Gluskap found his brother Malsum, who had followed him to the world, constantly working against him. Where Gluskap made plants that were good for people to eat, Malsum made those that were poisonous. When Gluskap tamed the animals so that they could be hunted for food, Malsum gave them teeth and claws to tear and kill. Gluskap fought against monsters and witches, but Malsum was in league with them.

One day, Gluskap sat alone in his wigwam, deeply troubled by the actions of his wayward brother. He knew that Malsum had always been jealous of his power and would stop at nothing to thwart him. Now his messengers, the loons, had brought news that Malsum was once more plotting against him. He would have to be on his guard.

A shadow fell across the doorway and Malsum himself entered. He seemed friendly and good-humoured and Gluskap put aside for the moment the thoughts which troubled him. Their talk turned to the many adventures which they had had and to the dangers which they had faced and overcome.

'We have been very successful in our lives,' said Malsum. 'I often think how fortunate we are, you and I, compared with mortal men, for their lives are so short and full of troubles. We never fall ill or grow old. All that can harm me is a blow from a fern root. Tell me, brother,' he went on, looking slyly at Gluskap, 'is there anything which you fear?'

Gluskap laughed. 'Only an owl's feather,' he said lightly.

'Indeed?' said Malsum thoughtfully. 'Only an owl's feather, you say?'

The conversation waned, and soon Malsum rose and took his leave. Gluskap's face grew sad once more. It seemed that Malsum meant to kill him. He sat late into the night, pondering on what he should do.

Next morning, he was awakened by the sound of Malsum's voice, calling him from outside the wigwam. As he stepped through the doorway, he saw Malsum facing him on the other side of the clearing. Malsum grinned evilly and raised his bow. An arrow tipped with an owl's feather struck Gluskap full on the breast and he dropped to the ground, pretending to be dead. He heard his brother cry exultantly, 'The great Gluskap is no more! Now I am the most powerful in the land!' And Malsum bounded into the forest, shouting in triumph.

When he had gone, Gluskap rose to his feet and said softly, 'It was well that I did not tell my brother the truth. No owl's feather can harm me. Only a flowering reed can cause my death and none knows that but I!'

In this he was mistaken, however, for he had failed to notice a toad squatting among the roots of a nearby tree. When he heard Gluskap's words, the toad hastened to tell Malsum.

He found Malsum sitting outside his wigwam, beating his drum and singing loudly in praise of his own might and cunning.

'You have been tricked!' cried the toad. 'Gluskap is not dead!'

Malsum stopped beating his drum and looked at the toad fiercely. 'You are lying!' he shouted. 'I saw him fall when the owl's feather struck him!'

'I have just come from him,' said the toad. 'He is as full of life as you are!'

Malsum threw his drum aside in vexation and began to howl with rage.

'But wait!' said the toad. 'I know what *can* kill him!' He puffed himself up with importance.

'What is it?' cried Malsum eagerly. 'I must know at once!'

'If I tell you,' said the toad, 'will you grant me my dearest wish?'

'Of course!' replied Malsum. 'But first tell me what you know.'

'Well,' said the toad, 'the only thing that can kill Gluskap is . . .' he paused for effect, 'a flowering reed!' he finished triumphantly.

'So!' shouted Malsum. 'Then I will find one immediately!'

'Just a moment!' cried the toad. 'Before you go, what about my wish?'

'What do you want?' asked Malsum impatiently.

The toad smiled dreamily. 'I would like to have wings,' he said. 'I am tired of always hopping on the ground. I want to fly and see the world.'

Malsum looked at the toad and his shoulders began to shake. 'What?' he cried. 'A toad with wings? This is too much!' And he laughed until the tears streamed down his face.

'I don't see what is so funny,' said the toad pettishly. 'You said you would . . .'

'Oh, go away!' said Malsum. 'I am much too busy to bother with your ridiculous fancies. A toad with wings!' He disappeared into the forest, shaking his head and chuckling.

The toad was filled with anger at Malsum's duplicity and he ran at once to tell Gluskap of his brother's intention. Gluskap scolded him for his foolishness and told him that, as a punishment, he would remain always on the ground. The toad hopped away, full of shame and disappointment.

Gluskap found his brother on the river bank, eagerly looking for a flowering reed. So intent was Malsum on his search that he did not notice Gluskap pull a fern from the ground and creep up behind him. Gluskap struck him on the shoulder with the fern root and Malsum fell dead at his feet.

Since Malsum was his brother, however, Gluskap decided to revive him, but not as he had been. Instead, he changed him into a large grey wolf, condemned to dwell forever in the lonely places, hated and reviled by everyone.

Now that his evil and vindictive brother had gone, Gluskap was able to continue his work in peace. All the people loved him for his goodness and often came to seek his favours, although he did not always answer their requests as they intended.

Once three men came to him and asked him to grant them each a wish.

'I have such an ugly, croaking voice,' said the first. 'I want to sing more beautifully than anyone else in the world.'

'And I,' said the second, 'am so dull and stupid that people despise me. I want to be able to make them laugh.'

The third said, 'I am afraid of death. I want to live longer than anyone else has ever lived.'

This last request made Gluskap frown, for he did not like to oppose the ways of nature and it is nature's way that men should die when they grow old.

Nevertheless he said, 'Very well, I will grant you what you ask. Come with me.'

He led them to a clearing deep in the heart of the forest. He told the man who feared death to stand in the centre. Then Gluskap passed his hands over the man's head and laid them on his shoulders. The man felt his body thicken and his limbs grow stiff. He tried to move his feet, but they were rooted in the ground. Gluskap had changed him into an old cedar tree, gnarled and bent.

'Now,' said Gluskap, 'you will live longer than any man has ever done. Your trunk is so misshapen that your wood is no use for anything.

No one will come to cut you down or to dig up your roots. You will stand here for a very long time indeed.'

The other men drew back in fear and trembling, afraid that Gluskap might treat their requests in a similar way, but instead he gave each of them a small birchbark box and said, 'Here are the gifts for which you asked—to you, song, and to you, laughter. Take them and use them well, but on no account must you open the boxes before you reach home.'

The men thanked him effusively and hurried on their way clutching their gifts, but, overwhelmed by curiosity, each opened his box before he had gone very far.

At once the man with the harsh voice found that he could sing like a bird. He sang and sang everywhere he went. He could not stop singing. Even when he went hunting, songs poured from his lips, frightening away the animals so that he never caught anything. For a time he managed to live on nuts and berries, but when winter came he had nothing at all to eat and he starved to death.

The dull man found that he had become extremely witty and amusing and people roared with laughter at everything he said. At first they thought him very good company, but, in time, they found him a tiresome fellow, for he was never serious, and at last, wearying of his constant jocularity, they drove him out of the village. For the rest of his life he wandered alone, telling his jokes with only the trees and the stars to hear him.

Gluskap's gifts might have given these two men great happiness, but, because they disregarded his warning and opened the boxes too soon, the granting of their wishes brought them instead

only misery, loneliness and finally despair.

Gluskap remained among the Indians for many hundreds of years, and those who obeyed him and respected his authority always found him kind and generous. There came a time, however, when Gluskap felt his power begin to wane. The people grew evil and treacherous. Even the animals no longer obeyed him as they had once done. Only the loons, his messengers, remained faithful. In addition, Gluskap was troubled by strange dreams and feared that bad times were approaching.

One day the loons brought him news of a wonderful sight which they had seen while flying over the ocean.
'A large island is floating towards our shores!' they cried. 'There are many people walking about on this island and others climbing among the branches of the trees. We flew low and looked at the people, but they were not like those we know for their skins were pale. We heard them speak, but we could not understand their language.'

Gluskap nodded sadly. 'All this I have seen in my dreams,' he answered. 'That is no island, but a great canoe from a land far away.'

He went down to the seashore and gathered the Indians about him. He told them, 'I must leave you now, for soon strangers will come among you to teach you of a new lord.'

The people were greatly distressed. 'Are you leaving us forever?' they cried. 'Will you never come back?'
'One day,' said Gluskap, 'one day, when the time is right, I will return.'

His stone canoe, so long unused, had already become an island, so he called a passing whale and asked him to take him on his long journey. He climbed on the whale's back and was carried out to sea.

The people stood on the shore and watched until the whale was out of sight. Then a great sadness settled over the earth. The people grew smaller and weaker. The animals withdrew into the forest and no longer sought the company of men. The loons, wailing mournfully, flew up and down the coast, vainly seeking their master.

The whale carried Gluskap far into the northern seas until at last they reached the island where the souls of warriors go after death. Gluskap leaped from the whale's back and landed on the shore. 'Here I will remain,' he said.

Sadly, the whale turned to go. 'Wait!' said Gluskap. 'Take this to remember me by,' and he offered the whale his pipe. It was old and broken, but the whale was very pleased to receive it. Gluskap filled the pipe with tobacco and placed it in the whale's mouth. The whale swam away, puffing his pipe, and Gluskap watched him until the last puff of smoke vanished over the horizon.

Gluskap lives still on the island among the souls of long-dead warriors. He sits all day in his wigwam, making arrows for his last great battle. When thunder roars and lightning flashes, the Indians know that he is angry. When they see the aurora borealis in the sky, they say that he is working late and, when no stars appear, they say that he sleeps. They look forward to the day when his work will be finished, for they believe that, when his great wigwam is filled with arrows, Gluskap will return to overcome evil and bring back happiness to the earth.

The girl who married a bear

Along the North-West Coast many strange stories were told about the spirits which inhabited the earth, sea and sky. During the long, dark winter evenings people gathered to hear these tales and to watch masked dancers act out the adventures of legendary heroes who had met with such beings or been captured by them.

The stories varied from tribe to tribe, sometimes even within a single tribe. While the Tlingit believed that it was Raven who had formed the world and made things as they are, some of the Kwakiutl claimed that it had been by the sun, whom they called Walks Over All the World. In Haida mythology the sky was seen as an upturned bowl covering the earth. Above it lay the Sky World, governed by a great spirit called Power of the Shining Heavens. The Nootka Indians, on the other hand, prayed to four great chiefs, each of whom ruled a part of the universe.

These spirits were the most powerful, but there were many others, both good and bad. Some protected people and helped them in their daily lives, like the Master Carpenter who could build a house or a canoe in a single day. Others were fierce, monstrous beings, like Bakbakwalanooksiwae, a hideous cannibal spirit, or the Thunderbird, a creature so large and powerful that it could carry off a whale in its talons. When it flew overhead, its wingbeats sounded like thunder and lightning flashed from its beak.

Because the Indians lived by hunting and fishing, animal spirits were particularly important. Many myths show animals taking human form, living in houses and behaving like people. Salmon, for example, were believed to be a race of supernatural beings who inhabited a great house under the sea. Each year they assumed the shape of fish and travelled far upstream to their spawning grounds where they died, their spirits returning to the salmon house under the sea. It was important that, after a salmon had been eaten, its bones were returned to the water so that the salmon could be fully restored to life. If any bones were damaged or thrown away on land, the salmon spirit might suffer injury and refuse to come again the following year.

Animals were often adopted as emblems, rather like family crests, to commemorate the roles which they had played in tribal myths. A Tlingit myth, explaining how such crests were first obtained, tells of a time when everyone lived in darkness because Raven had hidden the sun in a box. When Raven Boy let the sun out of the box, it ascended into the sky with such a noise that many people were frightened and ran into the sea or the forest. As they wore furs and skins at the time, they changed into the animals from which their clothing had come. The people who were left behind adopted these animals as crests in memory of their relations, and their descendants continued to use these crests ever afterwards.

Other crests or totems, as they are sometimes called, represented animals or supernatural beings reputed to have assisted the legendary ancestors of the tribe. The people to whom these crests belonged used them to decorate their houses, clothing and belongings. On ceremonial occasions dancers wore carved and painted masks representing the crest animals and spirits, and chiefs and important men had them carved on their houseposts or on poles erected in front of their doors. Because the myths were well known, a stranger coming to a village could tell from these totem poles which families lived there.

In the Tsimshian village of Kitwanga there stands a tall cedar totem pole carved with the figures of a mother bear and her cubs. The legend to which it refers tells how long, long ago a girl from that village met a handsome stranger in the forest and found herself a captive in the village of the bears.

It was late summer and along the banks of the Skeena River the fruit and berries hung heavy and ripe. Early one morning, Peesunt, the daughter of the chief of Kitwanga, strapped on her carrying basket and went with the other girls of the village to pick huckleberries.

High into the wooded hills they climbed, gathering the plump blackberries as they went and laughing and chattering to each other. As the woods grew denser around them, some of the girls began to sing softly, as they had been taught, to warn the forest animals of their approach. They knew that bears especially hated noise and that it was unwise to disturb them, but Peesunt tossed her head scornfully at the idea.

'Bears!' she cried. 'Filthy, ugly creatures! I care nothing for bears!' At this, the other girls grew even more nervous and peered anxiously towards the surrounding bushes, but all was still.

The day wore on and, by late afternoon, the girls' baskets were full and weighed heavily on their shoulders. They decided to turn back towards Kitwanga before the daylight waned and they started along the rocky trail which led down the mountainside. Peesunt lingered to pick just a few more berries, then ran after her companions.

Before she could catch up with them, however, her packstrap broke, sending her basket and berries tumbling to the ground. Peesunt, muttering angrily to herself, sat down to mend the strap and refill her basket.

Once more she set off in pursuit of her friends. She could just hear their voices echoing back through the trees and soon she caught sight of them in the distance. Yet a second time her packstrap gave way and again the berries rolled in all directions. Peesunt could have wept with vexation, but there was nothing for it but to mend the offending strap once more and gather up the scattered berries.

It was beginning to grow dark in the woods. Even by straining her ears, she could no longer hear the voices of her friends and, despite her defiant words about bears earlier in the day, she began to feel a little afraid.

Suddenly, she heard a twig snap behind her and she spun round. A young man, clad in a thick bearskin cloak, was coming towards her through the woods.

'Are you lost?' asked the stranger kindly. 'It is dangerous to wander here all alone.' He listened sympathetically as Peesunt told him of her mishaps.
'Come,' he said. 'Give me that heavy basket. It is much too late for you to return home now. My village is not far from here. You can stay there tonight.'

Gratefully Peesunt gave him her basket and followed him up the mountainside. Soon they came to a village, set in a forest clearing. The young man led Peesunt to a large house in the middle of the village and, with a low bow, invited her to enter.

As her eyes became accustomed to the gloom, Peesunt saw a number of people seated around a fire, all looking at her with great interest and all wrapped in bearskin robes. At the centre of the group sat an old man wearing a crown of bear-claws.

As they approached, the old man said, 'So my nephew, you found what you were looking for.' 'Yes,' replied the young man. 'Here she is at my side.'

The old man looked at Peesunt. 'She is indeed beautiful,' he said approvingly, 'and worthy of being your wife. Be seated, my child,' he went on, nodding in Peesunt's direction, 'and have some food. My nephew, your husband, will sit by you.'

Frightened and bewildered, the girl did as she was told. For a time, no one took any further notice of her. Suddenly, she felt something tugging at her skirt and, looking down, she saw a tiny, wizened old woman standing at her feet. 'I am Mouse Woman,' said the old woman, 'and these,' she pointed around her, 'are the Bear People. Your insulting words this morning angered the Bear Chief and he sent his nephew to bring you here. Do you see all the other women in this room? They were also taken by the Bear People, just as you have been, but they behaved badly and were made slaves. You must always obey your husband and treat him with respect, or else you too will be made a slave. Do not try to run away, I warn you. The bears will watch you constantly and kill you if you anger them. But do not be afraid,' she added, as she saw Peesunt's lip tremble 'for I will look after you and teach you the ways of the Bear People.'

For a long time Peesunt lived with the Bear People. She noticed that, whenever, they left the village to hunt, they changed into bears, becoming people again on their return. Her husband was kind to her and she became fond of him and of little Mouse Woman, but she was never allowed to be alone. Everywhere she went she was followed, in case she should try to escape. Often she grew homesick and wept bitterly as she thought of her parents and her brothers.

Back in Kitwanga, the villagers were grief-stricken at her disappearance. Search parties were sent out and brought back the news that bear tracks had been found beside those of the missing girl. As the weeks and months passed, most people gave her up for dead, but her brothers felt sure that she was the prisoner of the bears and

50

remained determined to rescue her. With their dog Maesk, they had won great renown as bear hunters and they were certain that, in time, they would bring their sister back safely to Kitwanga.

For over a year they searched but, although they stalked and killed many bears all over the country, they found no trace of Peesunt.

In the Bear village, however, their activities caused great anxiety and distress, and Peesunt noticed that when the bears returned from their daily hunt, some were usually missing.

One day her husband said to her, 'Your brothers have been searching for you and have killed many bears. Now they are very near and will soon reach our village. I am going to take you far up into the mountains where they will never find you.'

The journey into the mountains was long and hard. It was winter and snow fell, making the rocky track treacherous underfoot. At last they came to a large cave in the face of a steep mountain. Here they settled for the winter and here their twin sons were born. They were strange-looking children, half-human and half-bear.

One day, while the bear slept, Peesunt sat by the cave entrance, nursing her children and thinking longingly of her home. All at once, she noticed four hunters, with a dog at their heels, trudging through the snow far below. Scarcely able to believe her eyes, she recognized her brothers and Maesk!

She waved wildy, but the men did not look up. She shouted, but the wind drowned her cries. In desperation, she seized a handful of snow and, forming it into a ball, threw it with all her strength down the mountainside.

It landed at the feet of her youngest brother. He looked up in surprise and at first saw nothing. Then he noticed the imprint of a human hand upon the snowball and held it out to Maesk. The dog sniffed at it and began to bark excitedly. Scanning the cliff-face, the brothers saw their long-lost sister waving from the mouth of the cave.

Maesk's loud barking had awakened Peesunt's husband. He looked at her sadly and said, 'I saw in a dream that your brothers would kill me. I thought that I could escape them, but now I know that I shall soon die at their hands. Do not be alarmed, for I shall do them no harm, but you must ask them to treat me with respect. Do not let them drag my body on the ground and tell them, when they have skinned me, to hang my hide up with the head towards the sun. Put feathers behind my ears and rub red ochre on my back.'

Then, changing into a bear for the last time, he went out to meet the hunters and, because he knew how much Peesunt loved her brothers, he allowed himself to be killed without a struggle.

Peesunt and her brothers embraced joyfully, while Maesk danced around them wagging his tail and barking furiously. The brothers, however, were dismayed to see that their sister's captivity among the bears had changed her appearance, for soft brown fur had begun to grow on her legs and arms and over her shoulders.

Their return to Kitwanga was greeted with feasting and dancing and the young men won much praise and honour for the success of their mission. Peesunt was very happy to be back once more in her own village and yet there were days when, playing with her bear-children, she found herself thinking of the Bear People in the mountains. She knew that she was no longer fully a human being. Indeed, she now found that she did not care so much for the company of people and she moved out of her father's house to a small one of her own, on the edge of the village.

One day, her youngest brother brought her some bearskins to make warm clothing for the coming winter. Peesunt stroked the rough brown fur and thought longingly once more of the Bear People.

A great temptation overcame her. She put a small bearskin on each of the children and wrapped a larger one round her own body. All three now became bears forever and, afraid that they might do harm to the people of the village, Peesunt took her cubs into the mountains. They were never seen again.

The people who lived in the villages along the Skeena River never forgot the girl who married a bear, nor the respect which she taught them to show to a bear newly-killed, and, because they now knew the proper ceremony with which to appease the spirits of dead bears, they became great and successful hunters.

Raven and the beavers

Although many North-West Coast myths tell how Raven transformed the world from a sunless wilderness into a pleasant land full of good things, others throw quite a different light on his character, showing him as greedy and dishonest and much given to practical jokes. It was Raven, for instance, who induced the thrush to sit so close to the fire that his breast became singed and speckled; and it was Raven who deliberately stirred up trouble between the heron and the gull in order to run off with their herring catch while they were quarrelling.

On occasion, however, Raven's tricks rebounded, leaving him covered with confusion and embarrassment. Flying over the sea one day, he saw an old man fishing from his canoe. Raven thought that it would be a splendid joke to steal the bait from his hook, so he dived to the bottom of the sea and seized the bait in his beak. The fisherman, feeling his line twitch, began to pull it in. Raven hung on to the hook and dragged it back. The fisherman tugged harder, but Raven dug his claws into the sea-bed. The old man summoned all his strength and pulled so hard on the line that Raven's beak was wrenched off and landed in the bottom of the canoe. It was only with the greatest difficulty that Raven managed to recover his beak and fit it back into place.

Many of Raven's tricks were prompted by his gluttony. Sometimes these turned out to have beneficial results, as in the story of how Raven first obtained that very important fish, the salmon.

It all began when Raven was exploring the islands now known as the Queen Charlotte Islands, off the coast of British Columbia. As he was walking through some woods, he heard excited voices coming from a clearing and, peering through the bushes, he saw four beavers playing a gambling game called lahal. This game was played with a number of specially marked sticks, all different. Two of the beavers concealed a pair of these sticks in each paw and the other team had to try to guess which they were.

The beavers all looked plump and well fed and Raven thought that, with luck, he might be able to hoodwink them into giving him a meal. He changed himself into a little old man and hobbled into the clearing. 'I have come a long way in search of you,' he told the surprised beavers. 'My father told me before he died that you were his relations and, that

if ever I were in need, you would take care of me.'

The beavers, believing that he must indeed be a long-lost kinsman, welcomed him kindly and, just as Raven had hoped, suggested that he return home with them. Naturally, Raven was not slow in accepting the invitation.

The beaver's lodge was large and well furnished. Cedarbark mats hung on the walls to keep out draughts and at one end, opposite the door, stood a large painted screen, apparently concealing their storeroom.

The beavers invited Raven to sit by the fire and one of them went behind the screen, returning in a short time with a large salmon and a dish of cranberries. Raven noticed with interest that the beaver's legs were wet and that the fish was very fresh. It was the first salmon that he had ever tasted and he found it absolutely delicious. As he picked the bones clean, he made up his mind to investigate the beavers' storeroom at the first opportunity.

Next morning the beavers rose early and gathered up their gambling bags. They told Raven that they had arranged to play lahal with some other beavers on the far side of the island. 'Perhaps you would care to join us?' suggested one courteously.

'Thank you,' replied Raven, 'but, if you have no objection, I think that I will rest here today. I am rather tired after my journey.'

'Perhaps we ought to stay and keep you company,' said another beaver. 'It seems rather inhospitable. . . .'

'Oh, please,' interrupted Raven hastily, 'think nothing of it. Do not go to any trouble on my account, I beg you.'

As soon as the beavers were safely out of sight, Raven hurried behind the screen. What a sight met his eyes! Here was no mere storeroom, but a large lake, bordered with ripe cranberries and teeming with fat salmon, so numerous that the very water seemed alive. Raven waded into the lake and scooped one up. It tasted so good that he decided to have another . . . then another . . . and another . . . By the time his hosts returned in the evening, Raven had eaten very well indeed.

The beavers noticed nothing amiss and next morning, still unsuspecting, they again went off to play lahal, leaving Raven to indulge his greed

once more. In no time he had caught more fish.

As he munched, he began to plan how he could take the salmon away from the beavers. 'It does not seem at all right,' he mused, 'that the beavers should keep such a wonderful treasure to themselves. Everyone ought to have a share—especially me!'

It occurred to him that it might be possible to steal the lake as one might steal a blanket. He rolled the lake up very carefully, tucking in the edges so that not one drop should escape and then, changing back into a bird, he carried it up into a tall pine tree. Being Raven, he decided not to leave immediately. He wanted to have some fun with the beavers first.

On their return, the beavers were a little surprised to find their guest absent. Their surprise turned to alarm when they discovered that their precious lake was missing too. They ran here and there, searching for it everywhere, tumbling over each other in their anxiety. At last one of them caught sight of Raven in the tree.

'There you are, you thief!' he shouted. 'Give us back our lake at once!' But Raven, safe in his perch, only jeered at him rudely.

The beavers attacked the tree with their sharp teeth, gnawing at it fiercely until it began to topple. Raven calmly picked up the lake in his beak and flew into another tree.

This time the beavers summoned the help of their friends, the bear and the wolf. While the beavers chewed at the wood, the wolf dug and scraped at the roots and the bear shook the trunk with his powerful paws. They felled several trees in their attempts to catch Raven, but each time the wily bird only flew into another tree. He enjoyed teasing the animals and seeing them grow more and more angry.

Finally Raven tired of the game. In any case, he was becoming hungry again and so, calling out a mocking farewell to the beavers, he flew off with the lake in his beak.

The beavers were not to be baulked of their property so easily and they set off in pursuit. Raven, looking back, saw that they were quite determined to follow and wondered how he might give them the slip.

Suddenly he saw his chance. A large black whale had just come to the surface of the sea and

was swimming lazily towards the mainland. Raven swooped down towards it. The whale, thinking that a tasty morsel was coming his way, opened his jaws wide and Raven flew in, straight down the whale's throat.

The whale's stomach was dank and gloomy, but it was full of the fish which the whale had swallowed and so Raven was able to eat to his heart's content. As he was also very partial to whale meat, he began to peck at the inside of the whale as well. Not surprisingly, the whale found this rather irritating and plunged about in an effort to dislodge this unwelcome intruder.

In his discomfort, the whale failed to notice that he was drifting dangerously close to the shore of the mainland and, before he realized what was happening, he found himself firmly grounded on the beach.

An Indian village was nearby and the villagers were delighted to see the stranded whale, for its meat was a great delicacy which did not often come their way. Quickly seizing their harpoons, they killed the whale and began to cut up the carcase.

From inside the whale, Raven heard the commotion and guessed what had happened. As soon as an opening was cut in the whale's side, he burst out with a great flurry of feathers, scattering the startled villagers on all sides. At the edge of the village he stopped to see what would happen next.

The villagers, after their initial fright, crept back to the whale and peered anxiously inside.

They could not understand what the great black monster could have been. Raven hid the rolled-up lake among the bushes, turned back into an old man and joined the agitated group.

'What is going on?' he asked.

The villagers told him what had just happened and Raven looked very grave.

'Such a thing happened once before,' he said, 'at a village in the north. It was a portent of disaster.' He lowered his voice ominously. 'Within a few days everyone in that village was dead!' The villagers looked at one another in consternation. 'If I were you,' Raven went on, enjoying himself hugely, 'I would leave here and seek safety elsewhere. Do not stop to pack your belongings. Go at once!'

The terrified villagers lost no time in following his advice. Raven, chuckling inwardly, watched their panic-stricken flight. Then he went into their abandoned houses and leisurely helped himself to their goods and provisions.

There was still the problem of the beavers' lake to be resolved. Raven changed back into a bird and, carrying the lake in his beak, flew up and down the coast looking for a suitable place to unroll it. As he flew, some of the water trickled from his beak and formed the rivers of the mainland—the Stikine, Taku, Nass and Skeena. Other drops fell to become lakes and pools. Some of the salmon fell with the water and made their homes in the lakes and rivers.

At last, in a pleasant valley, Raven shook out the lake and laid it flat. He was relieved to see that no harm had come to it, although it was now a little smaller than it had been before. Yet the salmon still leaped in its waters and the cranberries still glowed red along its banks. Raven looked at it proudly. 'Now there is salmon for everyone,' he said.

The beavers did not abandon their search for their stolen lake and they did at last find it but, lacking Raven's magical powers, they could not take it away again. Although they were much aggrieved at now having to share it, they decided to settle down there beside it.

They never returned to their old home and that is why, although beavers are so numerous along the rivers and lakes of the mainland, there are none at all in the Queen Charlotte Islands.

Only One, the great shaman

When performing their rites, shamans wore special garments and masks representing their spirit helpers. Kwakiutl and Nootka shamans wore headbands and neck-rings of shredded cedar bark dyed red. Tlingit and Haida shamans allowed their hair to grow long and shaggy and wore crowns of fur, claws and feathers. They all accompanied their songs with wooden rattles carved with the figures of animals and birds.

Shamans often became very rich, for those whom they helped paid well for their services. Sometimes they were able to pass on their powers to a son or a nephew, but, even so, no one could become a truly successful shaman unless he first obtained the help of the spirits. While many wished to acquire their powers, not everyone was destined to do so.

Once there were three young men who greatly desired to become shamans. They had heard that, far upriver from their village, there was a place called the Cave of Fear, where shamans often met. They thought that, if they could find this cave, they might learn the secrets of the shamans.

They set off by canoe at nightfall, travelling in great secrecy, for they feared that, should their chief and the shamans hear of their intention, they might try to stop them. All through the night they paddled, and at dawn they reached the Cave of Fear.

Inside it was as black as night but, as their eyes grew accustomed to the darkness, they saw before them a pit in the floor. It seemed to reach down far into the earth and the sides looked sheer and slippery.

Fetching a cedarbark rope from the canoe, one of the young men knotted it around his waist and the others lowered him into the pit. They watched as he disappeared into the darkness and for a few moments they heard nothing but the sound of their own breathing. Suddenly, a scream rang out from the depths below and quickly they dragged their companion back to the surface. He was pale and trembling, and angry red blotches covered his face and body.
'The pit is full of wasps!' he gasped. 'A huge swarm! I never want to go down there again!'
'Here, give me the rope,' cried one of the others. 'I am not afraid of a few insects.' But scarcely had he disappeared from view than his friends heard him shriek, 'Help! Help! Pull me up! Quickly!' When he

58

reappeared, he too had been badly stung.

The third young man now tied the rope around his waist. The others tried to dissuade him, but he said firmly, 'I cannot draw back now. If anything happens, I will tug on the rope and you can pull me up again.'

As the darkness of the pit enveloped him, he steeled himself for the wasps' attack, but nothing happened. All was quiet and still. Down and down he went, until at last his feet touched solid ground and he stood on the bottom of the pit.

In the pitch darkness he groped his way around the walls, wondering what he might find. All at once there came a noise like thunder and a door swung open on the far side of the pit.

A tall figure stood framed in the doorway. He wore a painted dancing apron fringed with deer hoofs and on his head rested a head-dress of grizzly-bear claws filled with eagle down. Silently beckoning, the stranger led the young man into a large firelit room and motioned him to sit in a corner. Then he himself sat down by the fire. At his side lay a skin drum and a pile of dance batons. The young man was filled with awe for he realized that he was now in the presence of the great chief who was the spirit of the cave.

The door opened again and a number of shamans entered. All wore dancing aprons and head-dresses of bear claws. Each carried in his right hand a rattle and in his left a white eagle feather.

The shamans ranged themselves in a circle around the room. For a moment they stood silent and motionless. Then one of them began to sing. The others took up the song, shaking their rattles slowly and rhythmically. The skin drum leaped up and began to move around the room, sounding of its own accord. The dance batons also came to life and beat time with the music.

Still singing, the shamans turned towards the young man. As each passed before him, he laid his hand upon the young man's mouth and he felt their power flowing into him.

When all had passed, the great chief himself rose and, stepping up to the young man, said in a deep, grave voice, 'You have been chosen to do what no one else can do, for you will bring the dead back to life. I will protect you and help you in your work.

'From now on your name is Only One.'

The spirit laid his hands on the young man's shoulders and looked deep into his eyes. Then he returned to the fire and sat down.

There was another crash of thunder and the shamans vanished. The chief still sat by the fire, but the light was growing dim. The fire flickered and died. In an instant the room was plunged into total darkness.

The young man tugged at the rope around his waist and felt an answering movement from above. He was pulled to the mouth of the pit, half-fainting and unable to speak. His anxious companions carried him to the canoe and paddled quickly homeward.

For four days the young man lay unconscious on his bed. A terrible whistling sounded from his house and none dared enter. At the end of the fourth day, however, people heard him singing and, when they crowded in, they found him sitting up, ready to begin work. He told them of what he had seen in the pit and of how he had received the name of Only One.

From that time onward he travelled all over the country, working great magic, curing sickness and destroying evil spirits. As the spirit had foretold, his greatest power lay in reviving the dead.

At one village which he visited, he found everyone bowed down with grief because a young girl, the chief's only daughter, had been swept away and drowned in a fast-flowing river. 'Bring me her body,' said Only One, 'and I will restore her to life.'

For a long time the villagers searched for the girl's body without success. It was not until the following spring that they found her skeleton, caught up in some branches overhanging the river. The chief, remembering Only One's words, sent messengers after him and he returned to the village.

When he entered the chief's house, he saw the girl's bones laid out on a mat. He put on his shaman's regalia, the head-dress of grizzly-bear claws and the dancing apron with the fringe of deer hoofs. He blackened his face with charcoal and hung a string of carved animal bones around his neck. Taking his rattle in his right hand and his eagle feather in his left, he began to sing the songs which he had learned in the pit. He closed his eyes and heard the spirit of the cave speak to him. 'Sprinkle ashes from the fire over the skeleton four times and it will be clothed in flesh. Fan her with your eagle feather and she will be revived.'

Only One did as the spirit commanded. As the ashes gathered on the bones they were transformed into flesh and skin. He passed his eagle feather over the lifeless body and, to the joy of the onlookers, the girl sat up, alive and well. Everyone was amazed to see what had been done by the great shaman and in gratitude the chief rewarded him with blankets, slaves, canoes and other costly gifts.

Only One's fame spread far and wide. Whenever anyone died, he was sent for and he brought many people back to life. One night he was called to a village where the chief had just died. Many shamans had tried to save him, but all had failed. Entering the house where the dead chief lay, Only One again put on his head-dress and dancing apron and began his songs.

At the end of the first song, he stood up and said to the assembled mourners, 'My spirit helper tells me that your chief's soul is now in the village of the Ghosts. With your help I will bring it back to his body. Fetch me a new cedarbark blanket and let everyone present sing as loudly as they can until I return.' He drew the cedarbark blanket over his shoulders and set out towards the graveyard.

Beyond the graveyard Only One came to a slow-moving river, spanned by a narrow wooden bridge. It was a dangerous place, for the river flowed, not with water, but with boiling oil. On the other side of the river lay the dark and silent village of the Ghosts.

Secure in the knowledge that the cave spirit would shield him from harm, Only One crossed the bridge fearlessly and entered the house of the chief Ghost. The Ghosts had heard of his coming and all were assembled there. Although a large fire blazed in the centre of the house, the air was chill and the shaman pulled his blanket closer about him.

The soul of the dead chief was sitting at the back of the house, the Ghost chief by his side. The Ghosts saw that Only One was under the protection of a powerful spirit and, although they glowered venomously, they drew aside to let him pass. Only One stepped up to the soul and said in ringing tones, 'Come with me and return to your village!' He guided the soul out of the house and back across the bridge. None of the Ghosts dared to follow.

The people were still singing when Only One returned with the soul. Shaking his rattle, the great shaman circled the fire four times, following the direction of the sun. Then he placed the soul upon the corpse and saw the pale lips part and the eyelids flicker. He waved his white eagle feather and the chief who had been dead sat up, full of life once more.

In this way Only One brought many souls back across the river of boiling oil. The Ghosts hated him because of his power over sickness and death and they held a council to plot his downfall. It was decided that the Ghost chief himself should pretend to be ill and ask Only One for help.

When the message came, the spirit of the cave warned Only One to beware. 'The chief will offer you his own crown and dancing apron, but these are garments of death. Spit on your hands and smear them over your body before you put them on or else you will surely die!'

Only One found the Ghost chief lying by his fire, groaning as if in pain. His attendants brought forward a large wooden box and set it before the shaman. Inside lay a crown set with human ribs, an apron fringed with fingerbones and a rattle made from a skull with a backbone for a handle.

First having protected himself as the spirit had advised, Only One put on the crown and the apron and felt them icy cold against his skin. He took up the grisly rattle and, shaking it slowly, began to move cautiously around the chief's bed.

Suddenly he heard the voice of the spirit whisper, 'Kick the ground by the chief's head and spring back!'

Only One did so and all at once the ground opened and swallowed up the chief of the Ghosts. The ground closed again over him and he was seen no more. The other Ghosts fled in terror and Only One returned home in safety.

Among the other shamans, there were also many who hated him, envying him his wealth and prestige and they too schemed against him.

One day a message was brought from the chief of a distant village. His son was dying and no one seemed able to save his life. Once more the spirit of the cave cautioned Only One to be on his guard, for it was a trick on the part of his rivals who hoped to entice him into their clutches and kill him.

'Go all the same,' said the spirit. 'I will watch over you and guard you from danger. No harm will come to you as long as you drink nothing while you are there. Take care that they do not trick you into tasting something.'

The great shaman entered the chief's house wearing his bear claw head-dress and his dancing apron. The young man who claimed to be sick lay on his bed with the other shamans gathered about him.

The chief welcomed Only One as an honoured guest. Mats were spread before the fire and a feast prepared. The chief ordered his attendants to bring water and to serve the great shaman first. Only One took the bowl of water but, since he guessed it to be poisoned, he only pretended to drink and let no drop pass his lips. The other shamans were astonished and dismayed to see that he was unharmed and that their plan had failed.

Passing the bowl to them, Only One invited them to drink as well. The shamans looked at one another with trepidation, but, under Only One's stern and accusing eye, they dared not refuse and they drank the poisoned water. Almost at once they were seized with terrible pains and within an hour all were dead.

After this, none dared to threaten Only One and for many years he continued working among the people, earning great love and respect. In time, however, he himself grew old and sick, and one day he died.

His sorrowing relations dressed his body in his apron and his head-dress of bear claws, and laid him in a wooden box carved and painted with his crests. His rattle and his eagle feather were placed by his side. Overcome with grief, the mourners cut short their hair and blackened their faces, and all night long they sat weeping around his coffin.

In the morning they decided to carry Only One's body far up into the hills to the Cave of Fear where he had first received his powers and there bury him.

When they approached the coffin, however, they saw, to their amazement, that it was empty. The box was filled with eagle down, nothing more, and they knew then that the great shaman had already gone to rejoin the spirit of the cave. It is said that he lives there still with the spirit, in his home at the bottom of the pit.

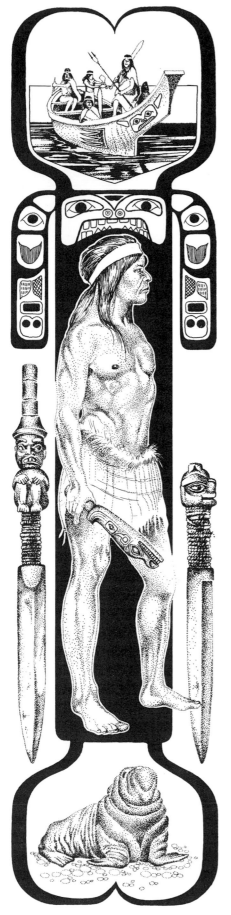

The strong man

A chief had four sons. The three eldest were brave, clever and industrious, but the youngest was exactly the opposite. Instead of joining the others in hunting and fishing, he spent the whole day sleeping by the fireside. Everyone despised and mocked him for his laziness and, because he was always covered with soot and ashes from the fire, they called him Duktuthl, meaning 'Dirty Skin'.

His brothers were very athletic and spent a great deal of time exercising energetically and engaging in trials of strength. Every morning, even in the coldest weather, they bathed in the sea in order to toughen themselves and increase their powers of endurance. As a result of their rigorous training, they were very strong and won with ease all the sports and competitions which they entered.

Duktuthl, on the other hand, appeared to have no interest in such activities. His brothers often taunted him about his cowardice and laziness and jokingly challenged him to a race or a wrestling match, but Duktuthl would merely yawn and stretch and go back to sleep. He was a great disappointment to his family.

Yet, all the time, Duktuthl was training secretly. Early each morning, while the rest of the household were still asleep, he rose and went into the woods. Here he exercised, running, jumping and practising with his spear and sling until he became very proficient. He chewed plants and roots known to have invigorating and purifying properties and bathed his body in the river behind the village. By the time the rest of the village stirred, he was back in his accustomed place by the fire and no one was aware that he had ever left it.

One evening the chief and his three oldest sons sat at the fireside discussing an expedition which they were to make the following day. They were going to hunt sea-lions at a very dangerous place far out to sea where only the bravest and strongest dared to venture. Duktuthl, as usual, was dozing among the ashes. One of his brothers stretched out his foot and poked him in the ribs.
'I wonder,' he said, winking at the others, 'where this powerful fellow will sit in our canoe?'
'Why!' grinned another. 'He will sit in the bow of course, so that he can land first. He will tear the sea-lions in two with his bare hands!'
They all burst out laughing, but Duktuthl paid no attention and

pretended to be as fast asleep as ever.

Next morning, when the hunters went down to the beach, they were amazed to find Duktuthl already there, waiting to join their party. His brothers shouted at him to go home, that he would be no use to them and would only get in the way. Duktuthl said nothing, but took his place in the canoe. In spite of their jeers, he refused to move and finally the little fleet of canoes, each with four or five men aboard, set out.

When they reached the island, they found a large number of sea-lions basking on its barren, treeless surface. The island was no more than a high, sheer-sided rock pounded by heavy waves and hunting here demanded great skill and dexterity. The trick was to wait until the crest of a wave lifted the canoe level with the top of the rock and then jump off.

Duktuthl's eldest brother tried first, but he missed his footing on the slippery surface and fell back into the rough sea. It was only with the greatest difficulty that he managed to regain the safety of the canoe.

The second brother then tried, but he too failed and was dragged back on board, dripping and angry.

The third brother managed to reach the rock, but he was attacked by a big bull sea-lion and hurled back into the sea.

The men in the other canoes were equally unsuccessful and at last the chief said, 'Let us go back. It is too dangerous today. We can try again tomorrow.'

To everyone's surprise, Duktuthl leaped to his feet. 'We cannot give up now!' he cried. 'We must fill the canoe with sea-lions! Everyone will mock us if we return empty-handed.'

'Sit down, you fool!' shouted his brothers, but his father, impressed by his unexpected spirit, said, 'Let him try if he wants to. Of course he won't succeed, but what have we to lose?'

Once more they paddled their canoe close to the island. As soon as the waves raised it level with the top of the rock, Duktuthl leaped forward and landed safely. The bellowing sea-lions crowded forward to attack, seeking to push him into the sea, but, as fast as each one came, he lunged with his harpoon and threw its carcass into the waiting canoe. Soon the canoe was full of dead sea-lions and Duktuthl jumped back aboard.

His father and brothers stared at him, open-mouthed, their amazement mingled with a new respect. That day they were the only ones to kill any sea-lions. All the other canoes returned empty.

In spite of this incident, Duktuthl's habits did not change in any way. He continued to lie by the fire all day, appearing to take no interest in what went on around him. Everyone decided that his success with the sea-lions had been merely a fluke and forgot all about it.

Not long afterwards, the village was challenged to a wrestling match by a neighbouring tribe. For days all the young men prepared for the coming contest. Duktuthl continued to carry out his training in secret.

When the day came, the men of the neighbouring tribe arrived in their canoes with their champion, a powerful giant of a man whose prowess in wrestling had never been beaten. The whole village assembled to watch and the contest began.

The first young man stepped forward and seized the giant round the waist, attempting to throw him to the ground. The giant effortlessly brushed him aside as if he had been no more than a fly or a feather.

The same thing happened with the next contestant, and the next, and soon all the young men of the village, including Duktuthl's three brothers, had been defeated. All were battered and bruised. Some lay where they had been thrown, dazed and bleeding, while others nursed a broken head or limbs.

The chief and the old men looked on shamefaced as the giant taunted them. 'Come on! Who is next to fight with me? Are you all afraid?' His supporters cheered him loudly.

At that moment, Duktuthl appeared, coated in ash as usual and rubbing his eyes drowsily. 'What is going on?' he demanded, stifling a yawn. 'Who is making all this noise and disturbing my sleep?'

His father eyed him with distaste and said bitterly, 'Don't you hear the insults that are being shouted at us? Who will avenge our honour now?' 'I will,' said Duktuthl mildly, and stepped forward to meet the giant.

Some of the villagers snorted contemptuously, thinking that this could only bring further humiliation upon them, but others said, 'Oh, let the fool try! After all, who will miss him if he is killed?'

The giant rubbed his hands gleefully. 'Is this the best you can do?' he roared. 'It looks as if the contest is nearly over!'

Duktuthl ignored the sneers and laughter and called out, 'Come on then! Why are you afraid?'

This enraged the giant and he rushed forward, intending to hurtle Duktuthl to the ground as he had done the others, but, try as he might, he could not move the young man one inch. Duktuthl stood quite still as if nailed to the spot, while the giant, grunting and sweating, strained every muscle to throw him down.

Then with no apparent effort, Duktuthl pushed the giant aside and stamped his foot on the ground. To the fear and amazement of the spectators, a powerful tremor shook the earth.

The giant backed away, puzzled and alarmed by this unexpected turn of events, but Duktuthl seized him by the arm and threw him into the air. He crashed to the ground several yards away, his back broken.

His crestfallen followers slunk back to their canoes, carrying their crippled champion between them. Now it was the turn of the villagers to taunt them. 'Where is the boastful giant now?' they shouted, 'Why does he not stay and fight? Come back, brave one!'

In jubilant mood, they turned to congratulate Duktuthl on his victory, but he was nowhere to be seen. He was found at last, nodding by the fire as usual, as though nothing had happened.

The villagers were ashamed of the ridicule which they had heaped on him in the past and now tried to win his favour, but Duktuthl ignored them, remembering their jeers and insults. Although his father invited him to take the place of honour beside him, the young man remained where he was among the ashes.

Soon another danger threatened the village. The spirits of the forest, where Duktuthl still trained and bathed in secret each morning, had been angered by the lack of respect shown to him and they decided to rise against the village and destroy it. Huge trees began to encroach on the village, crowding in around it. The people did their best to overcome the trees by cutting them down, but however many they destroyed, more came to take their places. The shamans tried all the magic at their command, but to no avail. Slowly the forest gained ground, pushing the village inexorably towards the sea.

At length the chief said despairingly, 'There is nothing more we can do. We must abandon our homes and take to the sea. Our canoes are our only hope of refuge.'

Just as everyone was packing their goods and preparing to leave, Duktuthl awoke and inquired sleepily, 'What is all the excitement? Where are you all going?'

His father said in exasperation, 'If only you stayed awake, you would not have to ask such stupid questions. Don't you see that the forest is pushing the whole village into the sea? We must escape as best we can.'

'Is that all?' replied Duktuthl. He rose to his feet lazily and went out of the house.

The trees were closely massed behind the village. Working with speed and vigour, Duktuthl began to pull them up, roots and all. He built up a barricade of trunks and pushed it back, forcing the forest to retreat. 'Go away! Do no more harm here!' he shouted, and at his words the trees fell back. Duktuthl returned home and went back to sleep.

Thus, for a time, the village was safe and life went on as before, but it was not for long. One day rumblings were heard from the distant mountains and violent tremors shook the earth. Fearing that their houses were about to crash about them, the villagers fled to the shore and, looking back, saw to their horror that the mountains were no longer distant. Like the forest, they too had been angered and were now gradually drawing closer, crushing everything in their path.

In a frenzy of terror, the villagers shook Duktuthl from his torpor and begged him to save them as he had done before. Once again the young man rose from the fireside and went out of the village.

The mountains loomed above him, dark and menacing, but, raising his arms, he cried fiercely, 'Go back! Go back and scatter!' And the

mountains did as he commanded.

As they fell back, they cracked and split apart, and from the fissures rivers gushed, dividing the mountains still further so that their power was destroyed forever.

Everyone was now very much in awe of Duktuthl, for they realized that, in addition to his prodigious strength, he also possessed great magical powers, such as could control forests and mountains. Tales of his feats spread to neighbouring villages and far beyond.

One day, a group of strangers landed on the shore in front of the village. Without saying a word to anyone, they entered the chief's house and went straight to the fire where Duktuthl was lying. Their leader said to him, 'Our chief is very ill. He wants to see you before he dies and has sent us to fetch you.'

Duktuthl followed the strangers down to the beach and climbed into their canoe. The villagers gathered to watch as it set off across the sea. Suddenly, they saw a great whirlpool open up before it. The canoe spun round and disappeared into its depths.

The canoe came to rest on the bed of the ocean. The strangers led Duktuthl to a large house where the dying chief lay on a bed of cedar bark. He was very weak and emaciated. On his chest rested the pole which supported the world.
'I am old and sick and will soon die,' he told Duktuthl. 'I have heard of your might and have sent for you to take my place here.'

Duktuthl lay down by his side and the old chief set the pole on his chest.

For thousands of years Duktuthl has remained at the bottom of the sea, bearing the world on his body. Now he, too, is growing old. When he is gone, who then will carry the world?

The Big Turtle

The Indians of the Eastern Woodlands accorded considerable respect to the spirits of the plants which they grew in their fields or gathered in the surrounding countryside. The most important of these were the Three Sisters who brought corn, beans and squash, and numerous festivals were held to celebrate the planting, ripening and harvesting of these crops.

For many of the tribes, the gathering of the first corn in summer marked the start of the new year. It was a time for dancing and games and for ceremonies of thanksgiving for the harvest. It was also a time for fasting, cleansing and new beginnings. Houses were swept clean, fires extinguished and old dishes and utensils thrown away in favour of new ones. Debts were settled, quarrels resolved and misdeeds forgiven.

Other ceremonies were held to invoke the help of the spirits and to drive away harmful forces. These were often conducted by secret societies, such as the Iroquois False Face Society, whose members wore grotesque wooden masks and carried turtleshell rattles. The masks represented the Faces, horrible bodiless heads which spread disease and destruction. By adopting the appearance of the Faces and by performing special songs and dances, the members of the False Face Society hoped to obtain supernatural power to aid them in curing illness and defending the community against misfortune.

There were other evil demons besides the Faces. Dwarfs, lurking in caves or in hollow trees, took delight in leading travellers astray or luring them into swamps. Forests were inhabited by fierce monsters like the nokos oma, a bear-like creature with long, sharp tusks, and horned serpents infested lakes and rivers. The Niagara Falls were said to have been formed by the huge body of one such serpent lying coiled under the water.

The sky was generally regarded as the home of powerful spirits who controlled the earth and who could be called upon to help and protect people. The name given to the ruler of the Sky Land varied from tribe to tribe. The Creek Indians called him Hisagita Imisi, the Preserver of Breath, or Ibofanga, the One Above Us. The Chickasaw linked their chief spirit with the sun and called him Luak Ishto Holo Aba, the Great Sacred Fire Above.

Many of the tribes believed that the souls of those who had led good lives went to the Sky Land along the Milky Way, which they called the spirit path or, sometimes, the dog trail, because of the legend that it had been formed by a dog dragging a sack of flour which spilled on the way. The souls of the wicked remained below in the dark and gloomy regions of the west inhabited by witches and demons.

The myths concerning the creation of the world are very similar throughout the Eastern Woodlands. It is said that, in the beginning, the first people lived in the sky, for the earth was covered by water and inhabited only by swimming birds and animals. It was not until an animal (or sometimes a bird or an insect) dived into the water in search of soil that the earth came to be formed.

The world was usually thought of as a flat plain enclosed on all sides by the great dome of the sky. The Cherokee, however, saw it as a floating island suspended from the sky by four cords. When the world grows old, the story goes, the cords will break and the earth will sink back into the ocean and all will be covered by water once more.

The turtle was regarded by most of the tribes as master and chief of all the animals and there are several myths explaining how he came to hold this high position. One, for example, explains the important part he played in the creation of the world.

In the days when water still covered the earth, one of the Sky People, a young woman, fell ill. The shaman, in spite of all his wisdom and knowledge of healing, could do nothing to make her well and at last he said, 'There is only one more remedy to try. I have heard that the roots of the wild apple tree contain a powerful medicine. If that can be found, it may help to cure her.'

The girl's father and brothers carried her to the place in the Sky Land where the wild apple tree grew and laid her down by the roots so that, if the medicine were found, it could be given to her without delay.

They began to scrape away the earth around the tree. They worked until their arms ached and they had made a great hole around the tree, but there was no medicine to be seen. They dug deeper and deeper until nearly all the roots of the tree were exposed, but still they found nothing. Tired and dejected, they climbed out of the hole they had dug and sat on the edge for a moment to rest.

Suddenly, with a rumbling like thunder, the edges of the hole began to collapse. The men sprang back in alarm and, even as they did so, the tree began to slip down through the earth. The girl, too ill and weak to save herself, tumbled into the hole and, together with the tree, disappeared from sight.

Far below, on the water which covered the earth, two swans were swimming. Startled by the roll of thunder, the first ever heard in the world, they looked up and saw the tree and the woman falling from the sky.

Fearing that she might drown in the water, the swans quickly drew together and caught her on their smooth white backs. The wild apple tree splashed into the water beside them and sank without a trace.

The swans bent their long graceful necks and gazed at their burden in wonder. 'What are we to do now?' asked one. 'We cannot always swim like this and already she is growing heavy.'
'We had better call a council,' said his companion, 'and see what the other animals can suggest.'

All the birds and animals that lived in the water assembled for the council. Big Turtle presided and for a long time they debated the matter, but without coming to a satisfactory conclusion. 'We must think of something,' said Big Turtle impatiently. 'I am certain that the woman has been sent to us for our own good, but the swans cannot support her forever and it is unthinkable that we should leave her to die in the water. We must find a place for her to rest.'

The animals were all very concerned and they tried hard to think of a plan. At last Otter said, 'What about the tree that fell with the woman? Perhaps there is earth still clinging to its roots. If we could find some of that, we could build an island for her to live on.'
'An excellent idea!' cried the Big Turtle. 'If we can indeed make an island in this way, I will support it on my back.'

Otter, who was acknowledged as the best swimmer, offered to go first and plunged into the depths. He was gone for a very long time. The waiting animals began to grow anxious, but finally, they saw him coming back through the clear water.

Otter broke the surface of the water, coughing and wheezing, but, to everyone's disappointment, he had found no trace of the tree in spite of all his searching.

Next Beaver went down, then Muskrat, then all the other diving animals. Each was gone as long as the Otter, some even longer, but, when they returned gasping and half-dead from exhaustion, all had to admit defeat. None of them had brought anything back.

It seemed as if the plan was doomed to failure. Big Turtle looked about him in despair. There were no more animals to send. Suddenly, a voice piped up, 'Let me go! Let me try to find some earth!'

It was Toskwaye the Toad, so small and insignificant that no one had even realized she was there. The other animals gaped at her in astonishment. Some began to titter, amused by the presumption of the little creature.

Big Turtle quietened them and said to Toad, 'Very well then. Go, if you think that you can do better than Otter or Beaver.'

Toad took a big gulp of air and sank below the surface of the water. The animals gathered close together and gazed at the spot where she had vanished. They did not really expect to see her again, yet still they watched. They waited for such a long time that they began to whisper to each other that it must be all over with her.

Suddenly, a bubble of air came up through the water and burst on the surface. More bubbles appeared, to be followed at long last by the small, ugly face of Toad. She opened her mouth and, with her last breath, spat out a few grains of earth on to the edge of Big Turtle's shell. Then she fell back, dead.

At once the animals began rubbing and spreading the earth around Big Turtle's shell. As they did so, the earth grew and grew until it became an island large enough for the woman to live on. The swans carried the woman to it and she stepped ashore. Still the earth continued to grow and spread until it became the world as we know it.

The Indians say that the world still rests upon the shell of Big Turtle. Sometimes, when he

becomes tired, he moves his feet or changes his position and then the world is shaken by earthquakes.

As for Toad, who gave her life to fetch earth from the roots of the wild apple tree, she is not forgotten by the eastern Indians. They call her Mashutaha, which means 'our grandmother', and no one is allowed to harm her.

Another story ascribes the turtle's supremacy to his bravery and cunning, and tells of a time after the world was formed, but while still only a very few people inhabited it.

One of these people was an old man called Kyehe, who lived with his young nephew. Each day the young man went in search of food and, on his return, his uncle would ask him what he had seen and found. Sometimes the young man brought back berries and nuts, but sometimes nothing at all, for then animals were not so easily caught, nor had men learned to make weapons with which to hunt them.

One evening, when the young man returned, his uncle asked as usual, 'Well, nephew, what did

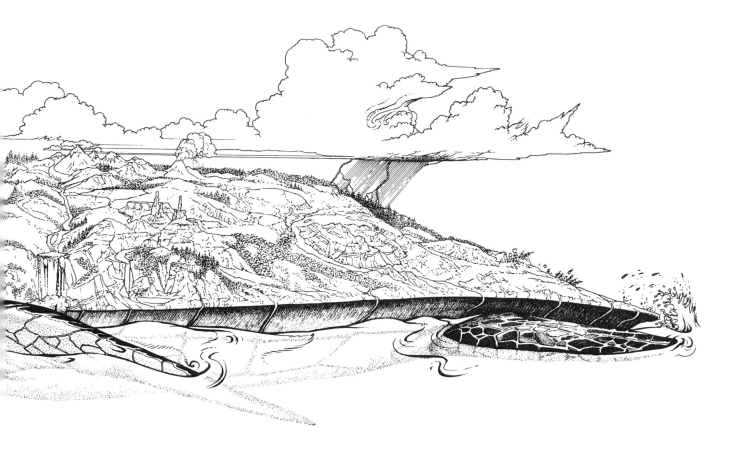

you see today and what have you brought?'

The young man replied, 'I found the Eagle asleep in a tree. I crept up on him and tried to catch him, but he was too quick for me. Nevertheless, I managed to pull out one of his tail feathers. Look!' And he held up the large glossy feather.

Kyehe was horrified, for Eagle was chief of all the birds, haughty and proud, and one who would not easily brook such an insult. 'What have you done, you stupid boy?' he cried, wringing his hands. 'You have put us in very grave danger!'

The old man rushed to the door of the lodge and looked up at the sky. In the distance he saw Eagle winging his way swiftly towards him.

He ran back inside and shouted to his nephew, 'Make haste! Hang the feather up in the smoke-hole. Perhaps, when Eagle sees it there, he will take it away without causing any trouble.'

Trembling, they crouched in a corner of the lodge. They heard the wing-beats come closer and closer, until at last they knew that Eagle must be hovering directly over the smoke-hole.

There was a long, terrible silence and they scarcely dared to breathe. Then they heard Eagle fly away. They looked up. The feather still hung in the smoke-hole.

The young man sighed with relief and said, 'He has gone without taking the feather. We are safe now,' but his uncle groaned, 'No, this makes it all the worse, for he means to punish us. The danger is even greater now. We must call a council.'

Not all the animals were invited to the council. The strong and powerful animals, like Bear and Wolf, and the fleet-footed, like Deer, were turned away, for Kyehe told them, 'You have no need to fear Eagle. Only those who, like ourselves, are weak and slow, are in danger.'

Thus it was the creatures who had most to fear, like Otter, Skunk, Porcupine and Turtle, who formed the council. Kyehe told them what had happened and warned them that Eagle would return for his revenge bringing his friends, Hawk and Owl, and all the other birds of prey. Each of the council members described what they would do to defend themselves when the attack came.

Kyehe's nephew said, 'I will throw stones at them and drive them off!'

Skunk said, 'I will spray my scent at them and tear their eyes out!'

Porcupine said, 'I will run my quills through them if they come near me!'

Only Turtle said nothing. He just sat and looked about him, blinking sleepily, as turtles do.

While they were discussing their courses of action, Eagle and his friends appeared in the sky overhead. Immediately everyone forgot his brave resolve and fled towards a tall tree growing nearby, each scrambling over the other in his haste to reach the uppermost branches.

Once more Eagle swooped down on Kyehe's lodge and hovered over the smoke-hole. The feather was no longer there!

The animals looked round in surprise and saw that, in the confusion, Turtle had carried it away! They watched Turtle plodding off through the woods with Eagle's feather clamped firmly in his jaws and felt very frightened.
'We must try to stop him,' they gasped. 'He will put us all in danger.'

Porcupine climbed down from the tree and ran after Turtle. 'Stop! Stop!' he shouted. 'You must return the feather to Eagle!' But Turtle kept on walking.

Porcupine was in a great quandary. 'Since he will not give back the feather, I had better help him,' he thought, and he clambered on to Turtle's back to try to shield him from Eagle's view.

As they travelled along in this way, Porcupine scattered ashes in an attempt to conceal Turtle's tracks. Unfortunately, the ashes had quite the opposite effect, only serving to make the tracks more conspicuous. Eagle and his friends had no difficulty at all in following Turtle and they soon caught up with him. Porcupine, fearing for his own safety, jumped off and beat a hasty retreat.

Seeing that he was surrounded, Turtle tucked the feather inside his shell and drew in his head and legs. The birds began to beat him with sticks, but that, of course, had no effect on Turtle's shell, so they decided to devise some other means of punishment.

Gathering some dry leaves and twigs, they built a fire and threw Turtle into it, but Turtle pretended that it was all a game to him, and laughed and rolled around in the flames as if he were enjoying himself tremendously.

Eagle was beside himself with rage. 'Since fire does not worry you,' he shouted, 'we will throw you in the river instead!'

At this, Turtle pretended to be very frightened. 'Oh no!' he shrieked. 'Not the river! Do anything else you will, but please, please, do not throw me into the river!'

The birds dragged Turtle, struggling wildly and pleading for mercy, down to the river bank and dropped him in the water. Turtle floundered about, howling as if in terror. Then he sank to the bottom like a stone and lay still.

Eagle and his friends, convinced that they had at last put an end to this troublesome creature, flew away in great satisfaction.

No sooner had they gone than Turtle swam across the river and hauled himself on to a log lying by the opposite bank. He pulled Eagle's feather from his shell and, waving it aloft, shouted, 'Kihe! Kihe!', which is the cry of a warrior who had defeated his enemies.

The animals hiding in the tree heard Turtle's cry of triumph and rushed down to the river to see what it meant. They were aghast to see that Turtle still had possession of the feather.
'We must make him return it,' said Otter.
'Who will go and take it from him? Porcupine, you go.'
'Oh no, not I!' snorted Porcupine. 'I have put myself in enough danger already. Let Skunk go!'
'I cannot go!' said Skunk indignantly. 'I might drown. Otter is the best swimmer.'

Otter was persuaded and swam across the river to where Turtle sat, proudly flourishing Eagle's feather. As Otter climbed on to the log, Turtle dropped into the water and dived underneath. He came up on the other side of the log and bit Otter's dangling tail hard. Otter yelped in pain and, jumping back into the water, swam as fast as he could to the safety of the bank.

After this, none of the animals dared to challenge Turtle and the eagle feather remained in his possession ever afterwards as a token of his superiority over all the animals and birds. To this day, the Indians claim, the turtle cannot be overpowered by anyone.

The wampum bird

Wampum beads, made from several kinds of shell, were highly prized by the Indians who lived along the Atlantic coast. White beads were laboriously cut from the conch shell and quahog clam, while the thick hinge of the clam provided pink and purple beads.

Wampum beads were used in various ways. They were strung together to form necklaces and bracelets, or used singly to decorate clothing, weapons and utensils. They also served as a form of money to ransom captives, to pay compensation for crimes and injuries and to reward shamans for their services. Most important of all, they were made into belts and used instead of signatures to confirm treaties and agreements between tribes.

The colour of the wampum was also important. White was the emblem of peace and good faith. Purple symbolized death, sorrow and mourning. White beads coloured red were sent as a declaration of war or as an invitation to join a war-party. Combinations of these colours were used to convey messages or to record ceremonies and agreements.

One legend tells how the Iroquois hero Hiawatha, while travelling through the territory of the Mohawks, came to the edge of a great lake. As he was wondering how to cross it, a huge flock of ducks descended on the lake and began to drink the water. When the birds rose up again, the lake was dry and its bed was covered with shells. From these shells Hiawatha made the first wampum beads and used them to unite the tribes in peace.

According to another story, however, the first wampum was not obtained so easily. An Iroquois girl had gone to gather cranberries in a marsh near her village, but there such a terrifying sight met her eyes that she dropped her basket and fled in panic. In the middle of the marsh squatted a huge bird, half the height of a tree, with fierce flashing eyes and a cruel, hooked beak. Its whole body was covered, not with feathers, but with purple and white shell beads.

The girl's tale caused great alarm in the village, for such a creature had never been seen before. The chief hurriedly called a council. All the wise men were summoned to find out what the monster was and what its presence meant.

The council deliberated long and hard. They prayed to the spirits of earth and sky and made offerings to enlist their aid. At last, the oldest shaman, the wisest of them all, rose to his feet to address them.

'Through my powers,' he declared, 'I have learned that the creature in the marsh is a wampum bird. I have heard that, in the Sky Land far above us, such birds do exist, but this is the first ever seen in our world. It may be that we shall never see another. If we can obtain the wampum which clothes its body, it will bring us much wealth and good fortune.'

'Then let us not waste a moment!' cried the chief. 'We must not let such a bird escape. I will call together my boldest warriors to kill it and bring the wampum back to our village.'

Led by the chief, the warriors set out for the marsh where they found the wampum bird feeding among the cranberries. White wampum covered its body, purple its wings. At a signal from the chief, the warriors rushed forward, shouting their battle cries and whirling their clubs.

The great bird seemed completely unafraid. It did not even attempt to fly away. Instead it turned to face them and, in spite of its ungainly appearance, it moved swiftly and fiercely, beating its wings and lunging with its beak and talons. So ferocious was its onslaught that the warriors fell back in disarray and retreated to the edge of the marsh.

The chief saw that the task of obtaining the wampum would not be as easy as he had at first thought. Already several of the young men had been wounded in the attack and blood flowed from deep gashes inflicted by the bird's sharp claws. He tried to rally his shaken warriors. 'Our clubs are no use to us here,' he said, 'since

we cannot get close enough to strike. We must use our arrows instead. Do not be discouraged. Remember what riches the wampum will bring. Moreover,' he went on, 'I offer an additional prize, for whoever kills the wampum bird shall have my daughter for his bride.'

The chief's daughter was the most beautiful girl for many miles around and her hand was eagerly sought by all the young men of the tribe. Each now swore that he would be the one to defeat the wampum bird and reached for his bow.

Arrows flew thick and fast through the air towards the wampum bird. As the first arrow struck it, the bird rose to its full height and shook it off. As it did so, the wampum showered from its body like hailstones and settled in great drifts around it. Yet, in an instant, new beads covered its body, as if nothing had happened.

Again and again the warriors drew their bows, but each time an arrow found its mark, the bird merely shook it off. With every movement, clusters of wampum fell to the ground until the whole surface of the marsh was covered with shining white and purple beads. Yet still the bird was unconquered and still wampum clothed its body.

The chief was in despair. It seemed that nothing could destroy the wampum bird and his men were growing weary and dispirited. As they discussed what to do next, they saw a young man emerge from the woods bordering the marsh and come towards them.

The warriors fell silent at his approach, their faces hard with suspicion. Several tightened their fingers around the handles of their clubs, for they distrusted strangers.
'Who are you and what brings you here?' the chief challenged the young man.

The stranger answered proudly, 'I am a Delaware. My village lies not far from here, beyond the woods.'

At his words, the warriors began to mutter among themselves. There had been disagreements and skirmishes between the Iroquois and the Delaware in the past and there were old scores to settle.

The young man paid no heed to their threats and went on, 'News came to my village of this monster bird. I have come to see it for myself and to kill it if I can. Clearly, it is no simple target.'

The Iroquois warriors grew angry. 'Let us kill this impudent Delaware now!' shouted one. 'He is an enemy and comes to mock us!' There was a roar of agreement from his fellows and they raised their clubs in readiness.
'Wait!' said the chief. 'Let him try to shoot the bird. If he fails, we will show no mercy and kill him where he stands.'

The young man fitted an arrow to his bowstring. None saw the arrow leave his bow and none saw it strike, but before their eyes, the wampum bird, uttering a harsh, unearthly cry, fell to the ground and lay still.

For a moment the warriors stood as if turned to stone. Then they rushed to where the bird lay. It was dead, the arrow piercing its head between the eyes.

The Iroquois looked at the young man with awe and amazement. There were still those who wished to kill him, jealous that he should have succeeded where they had failed, but once more the chief intervened and he was carried back in triumph to the village.

The wampum which had fallen from the body of the great bird was gathered up and carried back as well. There was so much of the precious material that even the largest lodge could not hold it all.

The chief was true to his word and he offered the young Delaware his daughter's hand in marriage as a reward for killing the wampum bird. The young man was as handsome as the girl was beautiful and both were well satisfied with the arrangement.

Then the chief said to the young man, 'Go, return to your village and bring all your people back for a great council. The Delaware have been our enemies, but henceforth they will be our friends.'

At the council the Iroquois acknowledged the Delaware as their kinsmen and, to confirm the bond between them, they passed back and forth strings of wampum taken from the body of the bird which the Delaware youth had killed. Ever afterwards the Iroquois and the Delaware lived side by side in peace and friendship and, from that time, no treaty was ever concluded without the passing of a wampum belt.

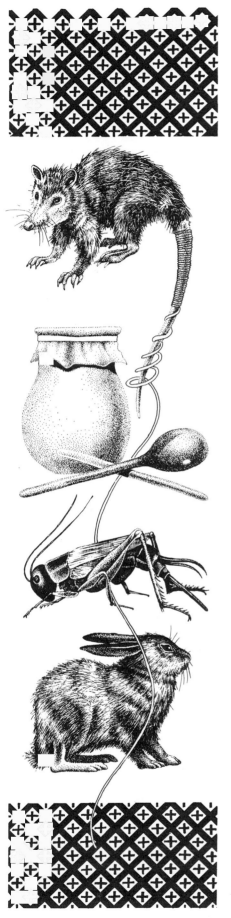

Why the opossum's tail is bare

It must be remembered that the animals which appear in Indian myths and legends are not the same as those which exist now. When the world began, animals were much bigger, stronger and cleverer than their present counterparts but, because of man's cruelty and aggression, these left the earth and took the rainbow path to Galunlati, the Sky Land, where they still remain. The animals which came after them—those we know today—are but poor, weak imitations of those first creatures.

In the beginning, before this happened, all living things—men, animals, plants and trees—spoke the same language and behaved in much the same way. Animals, like people, were organized into tribes. They had chiefs, lived in houses, held councils and ceremonies.

Many animals had characteristics which we would not recognize today. The rabbit, for example, was fierce, bold and cunning, and a great mischief maker. It was through Rabbit's tricks that the deer lost his sharp wolf-like teeth, the buzzard his handsome topknot of feathers and the opossum his long, bushy tail.

Opossum was very proud of his tail which, in those days, was covered with thick black fur. He spent long hours cleaning and brushing it and composing songs about its beauty and vigour. Sometimes, when he walked through the village, he carried his tail erect, like a banner rippling in the breeze. At other times, he swept it low behind him, like a train. It was useful as well as beautiful, for when Opossum lay down to sleep, he tucked it under him to make a soft bed, and in cold weather he folded it over his body to keep himself warm.

Rabbit was very jealous of Opossum's tail. He, too, had once had a long bushy tail but, during the course of a fight with Bear, he had lost most of it and now had only a short fluffy tuft. The sight of Opossum strutting before the other animals and swirling his tail ostentatiously, filled Rabbit with rage and he made up his mind to play a trick on him at the first opportunity.

At this time, when the animals still lived harmoniously together, each had his appointed station and duty. Thus, Frog was leader in the council and Rabbit, because of his speed, was employed to carry messages and announcements to the others.

As was their custom from time to time, the animals decided to hold a

great council to discuss important matters and Rabbit, as usual, was given the task of arranging the gathering and delivering the invitations. Councils were also occasions for feasting and dancing and Rabbit saw a way of bringing about Opossum's downfall.

When Rabbit arrived with the news of the meeting, Opossum was sitting by the door of his lodge engaged in his favourite occupation—grooming his tail.

'I come to call you to the great council tomorrow, brother Opossum,' said Rabbit. 'Will you attend and join in the dance?'

'Only if I am given a special seat,' replied the conceited Opossum, carefully smoothing some untidy hairs at the tip of his tail. 'After all,' he went on, grinning maliciously at Rabbit, 'I have such a beautiful long tail that I ought to sit where everyone can see and admire it.'

Rabbit was almost beside himself with fury, but he pretended not to notice the jibe and said, 'But of course, brother Opossum! I will personally see to it that you have the best seat in the council lodge, and I will also send someone to dress your tail specially for the dance.'

Opossum was delighted by this suggestion and Rabbit left him singing the praises of his tail even more loudly than usual.

Next, Rabbit called on the cricket, whom Indians call the barber, because of his fame as an expert hair-cutter. Cricket listened with growing amazement as Rabbit recounted his conversation with Opossum. Like all the other animals, he found Opossum's vanity and arrogance very tiresome.

He began to protest, but Rabbit held up a paw and said, 'Wait a moment. I have a plan and I need your help. Listen . . .,' and he dropped his voice as he told Cricket what he wanted him to do.

Early next morning Cricket presented himself at Opossum's door and said that he had been sent by Rabbit to prepare the famous tail for the council that evening. Opossum made himself comfortable on the floor and stretched out his tail. Cricket began to comb it gently.

'I will wrap this red cord round your tail as I comb it,' he explained, 'so that it will remain smooth and neat for the dance tonight.'

Opossum found Cricket's ministrations so soothing that he fell asleep, awakening just as Cricket was tying the final knot in the red cord which now completely swathed his tail.

'I will keep it bound up until the very last moment,' thought Opossum gleefully. 'How envious the others will be when I finally reveal it in all its beauty!'

That evening, his tail still tightly wrapped in the red cord, Opossum marched into the council lodge and was led to his special seat by a strangely obsequious Rabbit.

Soon it was time for the dancing to take place. The drums and rattles began to sound. Opossum stood up, loosened the cord from his tail and stepped proudly into the centre of the floor. He began to sing.

'Look at my beautiful tail!' he sang as he circled the floor. 'See how it sweeps the ground!'

There was a great shout from the audience and some of the animals began to applaud.

'How they admire me!' thought Opossum and he continued dancing and singing loudly. 'See how my tail gleams in the firelight!'

Again everyone shouted and cheered. Opossum began to have just the merest suspicion that all was not quite as it should be. Was there possibly a hint of mockery in their voices? He dismissed such an absurd idea and continued dancing.

'My tail is stronger than the eagle's, more lustrous than the raven's!'

At this the animals shrieked so loudly that Opossum stopped in his tracks and looked at them. To his astonishment and chagrin they were all convulsed with laughter, some leaning weakly on their neighbours' shoulders, others rolling on the ground in their mirth. Several were pointing at his tail.

Bewildered, Opossum looked down and saw to his horror that his tail, his beautiful, thick, glossy tail, was now bald and scaly like that of a lizard. Nothing remained of its former glory. While pretending to comb it, the wily Cricket had snipped off every single hair.

Opossum was so overcome with shame and confusion that he could not utter a sound. Instead he rolled over helplessly on his back, grimacing with embarrassment, just as opossums still do today, when taken by surprise.

The Morning Star

The tribes who lived on the Great Plains of North America believed that supernatural power was to be found in everything around them. It was in the wind, rain, thunder and other forces of nature. It was in the sun, moon and stars, and in animals and birds. The Sioux Indians called this all-pervading power Wakan Tanka, the Great Mystery.

For the Sioux, it was Wakan Tanka who was the creator and controller of the universe, but other tribes had their own tales about how the world had come into being. According to Crow myth, for example, the whole world had originally been covered with a sheet of water. There had been nothing at all until Old Man Coyote sent down birds into the depths to fetch mud from which he formed the earth. The Pawnee believed that Tirawa, the spirit who dwelled in the highest part of the heavens, had created all things by sending his messengers, Wind, Cloud, Thunder and Lightning, to shape the world, sow seeds and make rivers.

The Indians believed that these beings not only controlled the natural world, but could also use their powers to benefit mankind. If men practised the proper rituals to honour and please the spirits, they would gain power themselves and be able to perform great exploits in hunting and war. Gifts and prayers were offered to the spirits in order to obtain their good will and to bring happiness and prosperity to the tribe.

All sorts of customs and ceremonies were claimed to have been received from the spirits in dreams and visions. There were ceremonies to make a man invincible in battle, to help him steal horses or call buffalo. Many of these ceremonies were carried out by the warrior societies to which most of the men of the tribe belonged. The members of these societies protected their village against enemy attack and formed war parties to raid other villages. They organized communal buffalo hunts and sometimes acted as a police force to keep law and order in the camps. For their ceremonies they wore elaborate costumes and face paint and performed spectacular dances before the rest of the tribe.

For many of the Plains tribes, the most important ceremony was that held each year in spring or early summer when the tribe came together after the winter. The Sioux name for this ceremony was Dance Facing the Sun and, because of this, white men called it the Sun Dance. Despite this name, it was not held to worship the sun, but because someone who had been in trouble during the previous year had pledged to sponsor such a ceremony if the spirits came to his aid.

It was a very complicated ritual in which every movement had a special meaning. First, a Sun Dance Lodge had to be built. Then a tall tree was felled and set up in the camp. A bundle of twigs, buffalo skin and offerings was placed in the forks at the top of the tree. This was said to represent the nest of an eagle or thunderbird.

The dance itself usually lasted several days. During that time, the dancers, neither eating nor drinking, circled the pole, gazing steadfastly at its top and praying for power. Some, in order to win the sympathy of the spirits, tortured themselves, piercing their skin with skewers or cutting off a finger. Often, through hunger, pain and exhaustion, they gained the vision which they sought.

The Indians explained the origins of such ceremonies in their myths. The Sun Dance, it was said, was first brought to the plains by a poor orphan boy, the offspring of a star and a human girl, who travelled to the Star Country and was instructed in its mysteries by the great Sun himself.

It was a warm summer's night and many of the Indians had forsaken their airless tipis to sleep under the open sky among the cool, sweet-smelling prairie grass. One, a young girl called Feather Woman, awoke early. It was not yet dawn and the morning star had just begun to rise above the distant horizon. The girl propped herself on one elbow and watched the star as it climbed steadily into the dark sky. She thought that she had never seen anything quite so beautiful.

'I love the morning star,' she whispered to herself. 'How clear and bright it is! If only I could find a husband half as handsome as that star, how happy I should be!' Her loving gaze followed the star until it faded into the paler light of the coming day.

The camp was busy that summer. The buffalo were plentiful and there was always meat to be cooked and dried, and skins to be dressed and made into warm clothing for the winter. There was little time to be fanciful and Feather Woman thought no more about the morning star.

She thought no more, that is, until one day in autumn when she left the camp to collect firewood. Intent on her task, she wandered far from the camp. Suddenly, she became aware that she was no longer alone. A young man, a stranger, stood before her. He was tall and handsome, dressed in a robe of soft white buckskin embroidered with porcupine quills. He wore eagle feathers in his hair and, in one hand, he carried a small juniper bush festooned with cobwebs.

Startled, Feather Woman turned to flee, but the young man caught her arm and said gently, 'Wait, Feather Woman, do you not recognize me? I am Morning Star. One night in summer I looked down and saw you lying among the grass by your tipi. I fell in love with you then and I heard you say that you loved me too. Do not return to your village. Forget your own people. Come with me now to the sky, to the land of the Star People.'

Feather Woman looked at him shyly and knew that she loved him now as she had loved him on that summer night when she had watched him rise, bright and shining, into the sky, and, although it grieved her to leave her parents and friends with no word of farewell, she agreed to go with him as he asked.

Morning Star laid the juniper bush on the ground before her. He told her to place her feet on the lowest strand of the cobweb and to close her eyes tightly. Feather Woman felt herself being carried swiftly upwards and, when she reopened her eyes, she found herself in the Star Country, Morning Star by her side.

It was a land very like the earth below. On all sides the grassy plains rolled away to meet the distant hills. Here and there lay circles of tipis, the smoke from their campfires drifting into the clear air.

Morning Star pointed to a tipi which stood nearby. 'That is the lodge of Spider Man,' he said. 'It is he who weaves the ladders by which the Star People travel between earth and sky. Tread warily here, lest you damage his webs.' Then he led Feather Woman to the large, splendid tipi which was the home of his parents, Sun and Moon.

As it was still day, Sun was on his travels, but Moon was at home and welcomed her son's bride kindly, offering her refreshment of water and berries. While Feather Woman ate, however, Moon drew Morning Star aside.
'I fear that your father will not approve of this marriage,' she said with a worried frown. 'Take care that she does not anger him, for he is a stern man and will not hesitate to banish her if she does wrong.'

When Sun returned in the evening, he was indeed far from pleased to see his son's new wife. He had no very high opinion of the Earth People, considering them weak and stupid, but, despite his misgivings, he greeted Feather Woman courteously. 'Learn our customs, daughter,' he said gruffly, 'and obey our laws, and you will be happy here.'

Feather Woman was nervous of Sun, but she grew to love the kind and gentle Moon. Moon instructed her in all the ways of the Star People. She taught her how to tan deerskins so that they became as soft and white as snow, and how to extract the juices of herbs and flowers to make colourful dyes. She gave her a digging stick of ash wood, sharpened and hardened in the fire, and showed her where to hunt out the edible plants and roots which nestled close to the earth—the wild potato and turnip, the camus root, the milk vetch and the evening primrose.

For a long time Morning Star and Feather Woman lived happily together in the Star Country. When their son, Star Boy was born, their happiness was complete.

One day, as Moon and Feather Woman were out gathering roots and berries, the girl noticed a very large turnip half-buried in the ground. It was so enormous that its green leafy top came almost to her waist.

Moon, following her gaze, said, 'Take care! That is one root which you must never touch, for it is sacred to the Star People and great sorrow and distress will come to anyone who tries to uproot it. You must leave it where it is.'

In the days that followed, Feather Woman frequently passed by the giant turnip, but, although she wondered much about it, she was mindful of Moon's warning and left it well alone.

One day, Moon fell ill. She lay on her bed pale and wan, and so Feather Woman took her digging stick and went to gather roots on her own. By chance, she found herself once more by the giant turnip. She gazed at it, speculating on what lay beneath it.
'What secret can it hide?' she wondered. 'Perhaps it is a great treasure of some kind. Surely it would do no harm to peep below, only for a moment. If I replaced it very carefully, no one need ever know that I had disturbed it.'

Her curiosity at last got the better of her, and

she drove her digging stick into the earth at the base of the root and pushed with all her might. She gripped the tall green top with both hands and tugged as hard as she could, but, in spite of her efforts, the turnip remained immoveable. When she finally paused for breath, it was as firmly rooted as before.

She was about to give up the struggle when two large white cranes swooped from the sky and landed beside her. 'Your poor digging stick will never move that great root!' cried one. 'Let us help you. Our strong beaks will soon have it out.'

Feather Woman accepted their offer gratefully, for she was not to know that the cranes were the sworn enemies of the Star People. One of their favourite tricks was to tear down the ladders woven by Spider Man so that the stars tumbled to earth and were killed. The Indians believed that the puff-balls which they found on the ground were the remains of stars which had fallen from the sky in this way.

The cranes began to lever and prod with their long, sharp beaks until at last the great turnip, creaking and groaning, was loosened from its bed of earth and, with a mighty crash, rolled over on its side.
'There!' cried the cranes triumphantly. 'Now you can see what lies below,' and they flew off, delighting in the damage they had caused.

Where the giant turnip had been, there was now a huge crater. Feather Woman knelt down and peered into it. Far, far below lay her old home, the earth. She saw the wide prairies, the woods, rivers and mountains. She saw men hunting buffalo and girls gathering berries on the hillsides. In the camps the women were tanning skins or preparing food, while the children played between the tipis. The smoke from the campfires rose up to her and she heard again the voices of her own people. Homesickness overcame her and she longed to return.

Night was falling when she finally turned away. She rolled the giant turnip back into place as best she could and, with a heavy heart, made her way home.

Her sad and guilty face aroused Sun's suspicions at once and he demanded to know what had happened. When he learned the truth, he flew into a terrible rage.

'I knew that no good would come of this!' he stormed, stamping the ground so that the whole tipi shook with his fury. 'Have I not always said that Earth People were not to be trusted? They are all the same, these creatures, constantly meddling in what does not concern them!' He towered over Feather Woman and she shrank back in terror. 'Well, my girl, since you like to look at the earth, you had better return there. You cannot remain here any longer!'

Morning Star and Moon pleaded with him and Feather Woman wept bitter tears of remorse, but Sun remained implacable. Feather Woman was banished from the Star Country forever.

Sadly, Morning Star led his wife to where Spider Man wove his gauze ladders. He put Star Boy in her arms and wrapped a white buffalo robe around them both. Spider Man fastened a strong line about her and let her down from the sky.

It was evening and the Indians sat by their tipis, resting after their day's work. Suddenly a boy pointed upwards. 'Look!' he cried. 'A shooting star!' and the people saw a bright light descending from the sky.

They ran to where it fell and there they found Feather Woman and her son, wrapped in the white buffalo robe. They recognized her as the girl who, long ago, had gone to gather firewood and had never returned, and they led her back to her father's tipi.

So Feather Woman came back to her own people, but she found no happiness there. She thought constantly of her husband and her home in the distant Star Country. Every night, with Star Boy on her breast, she climbed far up into the western hills and sat, waiting and watching, until Morning Star came into view. She longed to speak to him, but he seemed so cold and distant that for a long time she did not dare.

At last, she plucked up her courage and cried out, 'Morning Star, my husband! Forgive me! Take me back!'

Morning Star looked down at her. 'Too late, too late,' he answered sorrowfully. 'You disobeyed. You can never return,' and he went on his way.

Lonely and unhappy, Feather Woman grew paler and thinner day by day, until finally she died, her heart broken.

Scar Face and the sun dance

After the death of his mother, Feather Woman, Star Boy was brought up by his elderly grandparents. He was a quiet, shy child and often lonely. His face was disfigured by a strange scar and, because of this, the other children in the camp teased and mocked him, calling him cruel names. So it was that in time the name of Star Boy was forgotten and he became known as Scar Face.

His grandparents died without ever revealing to him his parentage, for they feared that, if he knew, he would try to seek out his father, Morning Star, and be lost to them forever. Thus, Scar Face grew to manhood believing himself an orphan, without a relation in the world.

In time, he fell in love with a beautiful girl, the daughter of the chief. She had many handsome suitors and only laughed when Scar Face asked her to be his wife.
'Perhaps I might consider your proposal,' she said ungraciously, 'if only you did not have that ugly scar on your face!'

Hurt by her cruel words, the young man sought out the shaman, who was old and wise and a powerful physician. He explained his problem and asked him if he could rid him of the scar.

The old man shook his head. 'I do not have that power,' he said. 'That mark was put there by the Sun and only the Sun can take it away.'
'Then I shall ask him to do so!' cried Scar Face. 'Where shall I find him? Where should I go?'

Again the shaman shook his head regretfully. 'I cannot help you in that either,' he replied. 'I only know that his lodge is very far from here. They say that it lies beyond the mountains to the west. It may be that, if you went in that direction, you might find it.'

Early next morning Scar Face set out in the direction which the shaman had suggested. For many days and nights he travelled across the plains towards the distant mountains. In all the camps through which he passed, he asked where he might find the home of the Sun, but no one could tell him.

At last he reached the mountains and climbed far up into them until he reached the highest peak of all. For three days and nights he sat on the mountain-top, fasting and praying to the Sun to help him. On the evening of the fourth day, weak with hunger and exhaustion, he looked up and saw a bright path leading into the sky. It was the Milky

Way, which the Indians call the sky-trail.

The sight of it gave Scar Face new strength. He ran towards it and followed the trail until at last it brought him to a great open plain where stood a large painted tipi. A young man appeared at the door. His clothes were of soft white buckskin and eagle plumes were in his hair. It was Morning Star. The Star People do not grow old as mortals do, so he was as young and handsome as he had been on the day when Feather Woman first met him.

'What brings you here?' he asked Scar Face. 'Few Earth People find their way to the Star Country.'

Scar Face told him of his quest. Morning Star looked at him closely and at the scar on his face, and recognized his son, Star Boy, whom he had not seen for many years. He drew the young man aside to a quiet place and told him the story of Feather Woman and her banishment from the Star Country.

Scar Face listened with increasing amazement. He was delighted to meet Morning Star and to learn that he was not alone in the world after all, even though it seemed strange that this young man could be his father. He told him of the misery which the scar had caused him and begged him to intercede with the Sun on his behalf.

'I will do my best,' replied Morning Star, 'but I must warn you that Sun can be very obstinate and hard-hearted. Since your mother's disobedience, he has hated the Earth People more than ever. Yet perhaps I can persuade him to help you.'

In the morning, after Sun had left on his daily journey, Morning Star took Scar Face into the tipi. Moon was overjoyed to see him, for she had loved him dearly as a child and she listened sympathetically to his story, but as evening and the time for her husband's return approached, she grew nervous. She made Scar Face lie down at the back of the tipi and covered him over with cedar-brush.

Her precautions were all in vain, however, for as soon as Sun entered, he stopped and looked round, sniffing the air.

'I smell a stranger,' he growled. 'Where is he? Fetch him out!'

'It is only a poor young man,' said Moon anxiously, 'who has come a long way to seek your help,' and she brought Scar Face before him.

Sun saw the mark on his face and knew at once who he was. While Scar Face knelt humbly at his feet, Moon and Morning Star spoke earnestly on his behalf, begging Sun to grant him what he asked. In spite of himself, Sun felt pity for the young man's plight.

'You are my grandson,' he said at last, 'and so I will not harm you. But I put that mark on your face because of your mother's wickedness long ago and I am not yet ready to remove it. You must prove your worth first.'

In the days that followed, Scar Face did all he could to please his grandfather. He helped him in hunting and in all the work of the camp. Yet still Sun remained aloof and never spoke of removing the ugly scar.

Morning Star was proud of his son and they became great friends. Often Scar Face accompanied Morning Star on his circuit of the sky and they travelled far together.

Early one morning, as they were on such a journey, a flock of seven cranes appeared and advanced menacingly upon them. Morning Star feared these huge fierce birds, as did all the Star People, and he turned to flee, but Scar Face stood his ground. Using his buffalo robe as a shield, he struck at the cranes with his club. The birds attacked him viciously, but, although badly wounded by their sharp beaks, he laid about him with such force and energy that he managed to kill every one.

When they reached home, Morning Star told his parents of how Scar Face had saved his life and killed the cranes. Sun looked sceptical. 'I can scarcely believe that Earth People are capable of such brave deeds,' he said grudgingly. 'Show me their scalps—then I will believe it.'

Scar Face returned to where he had left the dead cranes. He cut off their heads and brought them back to Sun.

Sun laid his hand on Scar Face's shoulder and said, 'You have done well. Now that you have overcome the cranes, they will always fear people and attack them no more.'

Sun ordered a scalp dance to be held. The heads of the cranes were mounted on poles and, while Morning Star and Scar Face beat their drums, Sun and Moon sang songs in praise of Scar Face's exploit. Sun told him, 'Whenever the Earth

People kill their enemies, they should give a scalp dance and whenever anyone recounts his war deeds, praise songs should be sung.'

Then Sun directed them to build a sweat lodge. Moon gathered a number of willow saplings which Morning Star stuck in the ground in a circle, interlacing their tops to form a low, dome-shaped hut. Moon dug a hearth in the centre of the hut and filled it with red-hot stones. Scar Face and Morning Star entered the hut and Moon closed the door behind them.

Inside it was hot and dark. Morning Star poured cold water over the stones and in the steamy atmosphere they both sweated profusely, becoming cleansed and refreshed. When they emerged from the sweat lodge, Morning Star saw that the scar had gone from his son's face. As the two young men stood there together, both tall and handsome, they might have been mistaken for twin brothers. Sun turned to his wife and said, smiling, 'Come, Moon, tell me truly. Which one is Morning Star?'

Moon looked from one to the other in great confusion. She could no longer tell them apart. She pointed wildly and Sun roared with laughter. 'Foolish woman!' he cried. 'You are mistaken — the other is our son!'

He looked at Scar Face and said, 'Since you no longer bear your scar, you must have a new name. Henceforth you will be called Mistaken Morning Star.'

Sun presented Mistaken Morning Star with a buckskin shirt decorated with hair fringes representing the scalps of the cranes, and a pair of leggings on which were painted seven black stripes to denote the number killed. 'These stripes show that you have killed enemies,' said Sun. 'All the Earth People should paint such stripes on their leggings when they kill enemies.'

Sun then told him all about the sun dance which the Earth People were to perform when they wished to bring health and prosperity to the tribe. He covered the young man's face with red paint. He drew a black circle around his chin and put a black dot on the bridge of his nose. 'And that,' said Sun when he had completed his handiwork, 'is how your people should paint themselves when they make offerings in the sun dance lodge.'

Finally Sun placed a wreath of juniper on Mistaken Morning Star's head and told him to close his eyes. When the young man opened them again, he found himself back on earth, not far from his camp.

Mistaken Morning Star showed his people all the things which Sun had given them and taught them the secrets of the sun dance. He showed the women how to build the special sun dance lodge and gave them juniper wreaths like the one he himself wore. He instructed the men in the sweat-lodge ceremony and showed them how to raise the sun pole.

In memory of his mother, Feather Woman, he gave them digging sticks and made a special sun dance head-dress, hung with ermine tails and crowned with eagle plumes to symbolize the leafy top of the giant turnip.

His work complete, Mistaken Morning Star sought out once more the girl who had scorned him for his ugliness. This time she did not refuse him and he took her to live with him in the Star Country.

Often, near dawn, a bright star appears in the sky. People sometimes think that it is the morning star, but they are wrong, for he comes after, even brighter than the first. Thus, they can be seen together, Morning Star and Mistaken Morning Star, father and son, rising into the early dawn.

Behind the waterfall

The Cheyenne camp was pitched in a broad river valley. Although the sun was barely up, the day's activities had already begun. Fires had been kindled and thin spirals of smoke rose from the lodges. Women were busy with their cooking pots and men and boys were bathing in the nearby stream. Among them were two young warriors, Sweet Medicine and Standing On The Ground.

'Shall we join the hunt today?' Sweet Medicine asked his friend as he sluiced the icy water over his body.

'I suppose so,' returned the other gloomily, 'though we have had little luck for many days now – only a few deer and one or two rabbits.'

'That is true,' agreed Sweet Medicine. 'There is much hunger in the camp, and sickness too, I hear.'

The two young men hauled themselves on to the bank and gazed keenly across the valley, searching the landscape for any movement which might betray a grazing animal, but there was nothing as far as the eye could see.

Suddenly Sweet Medicine said, 'Do you see that hill over there? If we climbed to the very top, we could survey the country far better than we can from down here. If there are any deer nearby, surely we should find them.'

They dressed quickly and, gathering their weapons, set off towards the distant hill, following the course of the river. As they drew nearer their goal, they heard a sound like distant thunder and saw that the river was fed by a foaming waterfall which gushed down the rocky face of the hill, clouds of fine spray curling like smoke around it.

'What power the water has!' said Standing On The Ground in an awe-struck voice. 'If a man had such power, he could achieve anything, I should think.'

Sweet Medicine was silent for a moment. Then he said thoughtfully, 'Perhaps such power could be ours. I have a mind to see what lies behind that rushing water. What do you say, my friend? Will you come with me?'

Standing On The Ground was unwilling at first, but, not wishing to be thought lacking in courage, he at length allowed himself to be persuaded. Taking deep breaths, the two plunged together into the swirling torrent.

The water pounded their bodies and roared in their ears. Several times they were almost swept away by its fury, but they fought their way forward and at last, gasping and almost exhausted, they found themselves on the other side of the waterfall. Wiping the water from their eyes, they stood up to look around.

To their amazement, they saw, not the dripping rocks which they expected, but a grassy plain stretching far into the distance. Nor were they alone, for an old woman crouched over a fire nearby. She rose and came towards them. 'Welcome, my grandchildren!' she cried. 'Why did you not come sooner?' Why have you gone hungry for so long? I have food prepared for you. Come, sit here beside the fire with me and eat what I have cooked.'

The youths looked at each other in wonder. They guessed from her manner that the old woman must be one of the Listeners Under The Ground, the spirits who, from the very beginning, instructed the Cheyenne in their ways and customs.

The old woman placed before them two dishes, one filled with meat and the other with a yellow mush. 'Here is buffalo,' she said, 'and here is corn.'

The young men ate the food heartily, for it was good and they were very hungry. Yet, however much they ate, the dishes remained as full as before.

When they had finished, the old woman stretched her hand over the fire and drew out two feathers painted red, which she tied to their scalplocks. She painted their bodies red and drew a sun and moon in yellow on their foreheads.

Then, pointing to the left, she cried, 'See the buffalo!' The young men looked and saw, galloping across the plain, great beasts such as they had never seen before, clouds of dust rising from their hoofs.

Again the old woman pointed, this time to the right, and cried, 'See the corn!' And they saw fields of growing plants, swaying in the breeze. The rustling of their unfamiliar leaves made a soft, whispering sound.

The old woman gave Sweet Medicine a bowl of meat and said, 'When the sun goes down, I will send the buffalo out of the hill. They will live on your plains and you will be able to hunt them as now you hunt the deer and the rabbits. As long as your people eat this meat, they will be healthy and the tribe will be strong.'

To Standing On The Ground she gave a bowl of corn, saying, 'If your people plant the seeds and tend the corn well, they will always have something to eat.'

Then she led them back to the waterfall and told them to return home. 'Tell your people that you have brought them wonderful things,' she said, 'things which will make them happy.'

When the people saw Sweet Medicine and Standing On The Ground approaching the camp, they knew from the feathers on their heads and the painting on their bodies that they brought good news. Standing On The Ground passed among them with the corn and Sweet Medicine followed with the meat. Except for one old man and one old woman who were told to wait until last, everyone was fed. Although there were so many people, still the bowls remained full. Finally, when each person had eaten, the food was offered to the old couple and they ate it all. At last the bowls were empty.

Standing On The Ground said, 'I gave the old man the corn last because, when corn is ripe, it turns pale and old men have white hair. The men shall plant and cultivate the corn so that it grows well and ripens in the summer sun.'

Sweet Medicine in his turn explained, 'I fed the old woman last because it is the women who shall prepare the meat of the buffalo and tan the hides.'

At sunset the buffalo began to come out of the hill, so many of them that the ground shook and many of the people hid in terror. All night they thundered past and by the morning the herds had spread across the whole country. The hunters who went out with their spears and arrows brought back more meat than had ever been seen before.

From that time on, as the buffalo moved, so the people moved their camp and followed them. When spring came, they planted their corn and in autumn they gathered the ripe ears. Thus buffalo and corn came to the Cheyenne and, as long as they had these things in plenty, there was neither hunger nor sickness among them, just as the old woman had said.

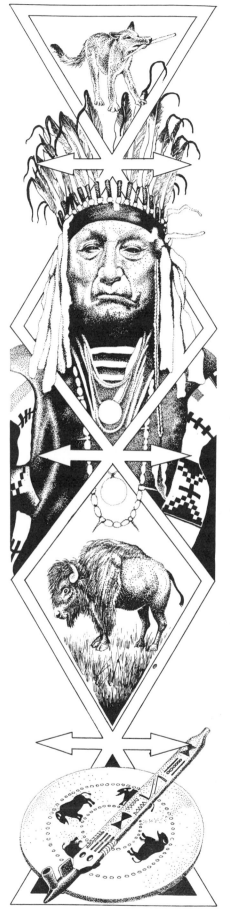

The search for the buffalo

In the old days, vast herds of buffalo, often several thousand strong, roamed the open grasslands of North America. The lives of the Plains Indians revolved around the movements of these herds, for the animals provided them with most of life's necessities. The meat was eaten fresh, or dried and stored against the long winter months when hunting was difficult. The skins, cleaned and dressed, were used for clothing, bedding, tipi covers, bags and riding tackle. Tools were made from the bones, ropes from the hair, thread and bowstrings from the sinews and cups and spoons from the horns. Nothing was wasted.

There was once a time, however, when the Blackfoot people were faced with famine and disaster, for no buffalo could be found. Day after day, hunters scoured the plains, but every evening they returned empty handed. The people grew thin and pale and the children cried with hunger. In despair, their chief decided to enlist the aid of Napi, the Old Man of the Dawn. According to Blackfoot mythology, it was Napi who set the world in order and caused things to be the way they are.

Napi listened sympathetically to the chief's pleas for help. Then he answered, 'Far to the west, beyond the Sweet Grass Hills, is the lodge of the shaman Crow Arrow. In my opinion, it is he who has stolen the buffalo. I know that he is jealous of the honour which you pay me and I believe that he has hidden the herds from you in revenge.'

'But what are we to do?' cried the chief. 'How can we survive without the buffalo? Already my people are weak with hunger. Soon winter will be upon us and there will be neither food to eat nor skins to keep us warm. What will become of us?'

'Take heart,' Napi reassured him. 'I will seek out Crow Arrow. I will find where he has taken the buffalo and restore them to you. Is there any among your people who is ready to accompany me on my search?'

The chief's son stepped forward. His name was Little Dog. 'Let me come with you,' he said. 'When I became a man, I went into the mountains and fasted and prayed for many days. Then spirits came to me and granted powers to aid me in times of trouble. Perhaps these powers will help us now.'

'What powers have you?' asked Napi.

'I have strength and courage,' replied the young man, 'and I can turn myself into a swallow or a spider or a dog.'

Napi nodded approvingly. 'These are good powers indeed,' he said. 'Mine are stronger, it is true, for I can turn myself into anything at all. Yet your powers may be of use, so let us go together.'

They set out from the Blackfoot camp and for many days they travelled across the plains to the west. When they came to the foot of the Sweet Grass Hills, Napi changed into a horsefly and Little Dog into a swallow and together they flew over the hills.

On the other side, they looked down on a wooded valley. A river ran among the trees and on its bank stood a lone tipi, the home of the evil shaman Crow Arrow.

Not wishing their approach to be seen, they again changed their forms. Little Dog turned himself into a spider and Napi became a pine tree. With great caution they made their way towards Crow Arrow's camp. Soon they were close enough to hear the murmur of voices and to smell the smoke from the campfire. Yet still they saw no trace of the buffalo.

The camp contained only three people — Crow Arrow himself, his wife and their little daughter. Napi and Little Dog watched the camp for several days, hoping to learn something that would help them in their quest, but in vain.

'Perhaps you were mistaken,' whispered Little Dog. 'Perhaps the buffalo are not here after all.'

Napi bent his head to catch the spider's tiny voice. 'I do not think so,' he answered grimly, tossing his branches. 'I am sure that they are hidden somewhere nearby. We must do something to get into the camp itself.'

After some discussion, they hit on a plan. Napi changed into a stick of ash wood and Little Dog into a small brown puppy. He began to yelp loudly and capered round the stick, pretending to worry it with his little sharp teeth.

His antics soon attracted the attention of Crow Arrow's little daughter. She ran towards the puppy and picked him up, hugging him close and stroking his head. She saw the stick lying on the ground and picked that up as well, thinking that it might be of use to her mother in digging up roots. She carried them both back into the camp. 'Look, Mother!' she cried. 'See what I have found!'

The woman was delighted with the fine strong digging stick, for it was just what she needed, and she put it carefully with her other tools at one side of the tipi. Crow Arrow was less pleased to see the puppy, thinking that he might prove a nuisance, but the child refused to be parted from her new pet. She played with the puppy all day and at night he slept in the tipi by her side.

In the morning Crow Arrow left the camp to go hunting. After he had gone, his wife picked up her new digging stick and went into the woods with her daughter to gather roots and berries. Little Dog trotted at their heels.

The day was hot and, after gathering a large quantity of berries, the woman sat down to rest under a tree. After a time she fell into a doze. The little girl sat beside her sleeping mother and played with the puppy. As she played, she talked to him.

'Do you want to know a secret, puppy?' she asked softly. 'I know a place where there are many animals, much bigger than you are!'

Little Dog pricked up his ears and looked at her enquiringly with his bright brown eyes. 'Shall I show you the place, puppy?' she teased him. The puppy leaped up and down in excitement, licking her face with his soft pink tongue and wagging his tail furiously.

'Come on then,' she said, jumping to her feet. Pausing only to seize the digging stick in his teeth, Little Dog scampered after her.

She led him to where a thick clump of bushes grew against a high rock and pulled the bushes aside to reveal a gaping hole in the face of the rock. 'Look down there, puppy!' said the little girl. 'Do you see them?'

Little Dog peered down into the hole and saw, in a great cavern below, the milling herds of buffalo, thousands of great brown beasts, pushing and jostling against one another. He could hear the snorting of the bulls and the stamping of their feet as they pawed the floor of the cavern.

The little girl had him tightly by the scruff of his neck, but he wriggled free and tumbled down into the cavern. The digging stick, which he had dropped in his excitement, slithered after him. 'Come back!' shrieked the child. 'You must not go down there! Come back at once, do you hear!'

93

Napi and Little Dog, intent upon the buffalo, paid no heed. The little girl was very frightened, for she knew she should not have taken her pet to that forbidden place. She ran back to her mother, who had been awakened by the clamour, and told her that the puppy had run off with the digging stick and that, although she had tried to follow them, she had lost them in the woods. Her mother was extremely angry and scolded her severely for her carelessness. She returned to the camp, with her daughter trailing behind her in tears.

Meanwhile, in the depths of the cavern, Napi and Little Dog had begun to round up the buffalo. Napi changed back into human form and the puppy grew into a huge dog and, with much shouting and barking, they drove the buffalo up the slope and out through the hole in the rock. The hoofs of the stampeding buffalo shook the ground and filled the air with a noise like thunder.

In the distance, Crow Arrow heard the din and realized what was happening. He rushed back to the rock in time to see the great herds burst from the mouth of the cavern, the dust rising like smoke around them. Powerless to halt their headlong charge, he flattened himself against the rock to avoid their horns and trampling hoofs. He could make out the shouting and barking within the cave and knew that their escape was no accident.

'I may have lost my hold over the buffalo,' he muttered, eyes glinting with fury, 'but I will catch those responsible. They will pay dearly for their actions!' He drew his hunting knife and crouched in wait.

But Napi and Little Dog were not to be trapped so easily. As the last buffalo pounded up the slope, they changed once more into a stick and a puppy and leaped on to its back. They burrowed deep into the shaggy hair and were carried out unseen. When the vengeful Crow Arrow at last rushed into the cavern, it was completely empty.

Driven on by their rescuers, the buffalo galloped across the valley, up over the Sweet Grass Hills and down into the plains on the other side. Here their pace slackened and they began to spread slowly across the rich grasslands, grazing peacefully. That night a feast was held to welcome back Napi and Little Dog and once more the smell of roasting meat rose over the Blackfoot camp.

Next day, however, as some of the hunters were driving a herd of buffalo into a corral, a huge grey bird appeared in the sky and hovered over the buffalo, frightening them with its wild, raucous cries. Napi knew that it was Crow Arrow trying yet again to take the buffalo for himself.

He went out of the camp and, turning himself into a beaver, lay down in the grass as if dead. The bird, thinking this an easy meal, swooped down upon him. Quick as lightning, Napi changed back into a man and seized Crow Arrow's legs in a powerful grasp. Ignoring his squawks and thrashing wings, he carried him back to the camp and tied him in the smoke-hole of the chief's tipi.

Here the bird hung all day, filling the air with his fearful cries and struggling unsuccessfully to free himself. By the evening he was a sorry sight, for the smoke from the fire had turned his grey plumage jet black.

Napi looked up at the dejected bundle of sooty feathers. 'Well, Crow Arrow!' he said. 'You see where your wickedness and greed have brought you?'

'Let me go, Napi!' pleaded Crow Arrow. 'I will not steal the buffalo again. I will bring you more. I will cause no further trouble.'

'Do you promise?' asked Napi sternly.

'I promise!' cried Crow Arrow. 'Only let me go! Let me return to my wife and child!'

Napi cut the ropes that bound him and, with a dismal cry, the bird flapped his wings and disappeared into the night sky.

Since that time the crow's feathers have always been black. Crow Arrow himself never again dared to threaten the buffalo and, until strangers with hard hearts and guns came to hunt them almost to extinction, the great herds remained plentiful on the plains.

The adventures of Iktomi

Many demons and monsters once inhabited the dark and lonely places of the Great Plains. There was Iya, who devoured people and animals in the form of a cyclone, and Gnaske, the Crazy Buffalo, who caused madness and disease. In the woods lurked the fearsome witch Anukite or Double Face. One half of her face was very beautiful, but the other half was horribly ugly.

One of the most troublesome of these malevolent beings was Iktomi the Trickster. He had lived in the Sky Land until he stirred up such dissension between Sun and Moon that Skan, the ruler of the Sky Land, banished him to Earth. The Indians say that it was Iktomi who brought all the evil things into the world and taught men to lie and steal.

Iktomi made mischief wherever he went. One day he met Rabbit out hunting. Rabbit was splendidly dressed in white buckskin with a robe of raccoon skin about his shoulders and Iktomi felt very envious. He sat down by the side of the path and pretended to cry.
'I am so hungry,' he sobbed. 'I have had nothing to eat for days. There is a pheasant at the top of that tree, but I have no weapons. What am I to do?'

Rabbit was very sympathetic. He drew an arrow from his quiver and let fly at the pheasant, killing it instantly. The bird tumbled from its perch and lodged in a branch lower down.
'How clever you are!' cried Iktomi, drying his tears. 'Could you climb up and fetch it down for me? I have injured my leg,' he lied, 'and I fear that it would pain me to do so. But wait a moment,' he added as Rabbit moved towards the tree. 'Take care that you do not spoil your fine clothes. Let me hold them for you while you climb up.'

Rabbit took off his shirt and his robe as Iktomi suggested and climbed into the tree. Iktomi stood at the bottom, telling him the best way to go. As a result of Iktomi's instructions, Rabbit soon found himself firmly wedged between two branches.
'Hey!' he shouted. 'I seem to be stuck. Can you help me down?'

Iktomi began to laugh. 'I do not see how I can help,' he grinned. 'You will just have to stay there. But it does seem a pity to let these fine clothes go to waste,' and he slipped Rabbit's shirt over his head.
'What are you doing?' cried Rabbit. He struggled furiously to free

himself, but only succeeded in becoming even more tightly wedged. Iktomi carelessly threw the raccoon robe over his shoulder and sauntered off, leaving Rabbit shouting angrily.

A little further on, Iktomi found his way barred by a wide, fast-flowing river. Noticing a hawk flying overhead, he again sat down and pretended to cry.

The hawk landed beside him and asked what was wrong. When he heard that Iktomi wanted to cross the river, he said, 'That is no problem. Jump on my back and I will carry you across.'

Iktomi seated himself on the hawk's back and they rose into the air.
'What fools these animals are!' thought Iktomi contemptuously. 'I can get them to do anything for me!'

In his arrogance, he began to mock the hawk behind his back, wrinkling up his nose and sticking out his tongue. The hawk, of course, was quite unaware of what was going on.

Iktomi grew bolder and began to snap his fingers at the hawk's head. To the Indians this is a very insulting gesture and Iktomi only dared to do it because he thought that the hawk could not see him. Unfortunately for him, they had by now reached the other side of the river. The sun cast their shadows, long and black, on the ground below. The hawk, glancing down, saw at once what Iktomi was doing.
'The scoundrel!' fumed the hawk and he began to look for a way to rid himself of his ungrateful passenger. An old hollow tree below gave him an idea and he swooped down towards it. As he passed over the tree, he tilted his body sharply, hurling the startled Iktomi down into the dark, dank hollow.

While there was room enough inside the tree for Iktomi to stand up and move about, there was little chance of escape, for the sides of the trunk were smooth and slippery. He was well and truly trapped.

Suddenly, he heard the murmur of voices. Peering through a small chink in the bark, he saw two women gathering firewood. At once his mischievous spirits rose.

Rabbit's raccoon robe still had the tail attached. Iktomi pushed it through the hole and shook it up and down. At the same time he sang loudly, 'Here

am I, a fat raccoon! Here am I, a fat raccoon!'

He pulled the raccoon tail inside again and looked to see what was happening. The women were staring at the tree, open mouthed.
'I do believe,' said one, 'that there is a raccoon inside that tree. I saw its tail appear a moment ago.'
'We must catch it!' replied the other. 'Raccoon fat is one of the best things for dressing hides.'

The women began to chop at the tree with their axes. As the tree was already dead and half-rotten, it was not long before they managed to push it over on to the ground.

Iktomi continued to sit tight inside the hollow trunk, partly because he wanted to go on teasing the women a little longer, and partly because he did feel rather sheepish at having allowed himself to be trapped in such an undignified way. Again he hung the raccoon tail out of the hole.
'He is still in there,' he heard one of the women say. 'How are we to get him out?'
'Make a fire!' warbled Iktomi in reply. 'Smoke me out!'
'Of course!' cried the women. 'What a good idea!' They both rushed back to their village to fetch some burning twigs from the campfire.

As soon as they had gone, Iktomi crawled out of the tree and made off through the wood, chuckling at his own cleverness.

Later that day, as he was passing through a clearing, he heard the sound of music. At first he could see nothing. Then he noticed a buffalo skull lying at the foot of a tree. He crouched down and peered through one of the eye-sockets.

Inside, a party of mice were having a dance. They skipped about in their most splendid costumes, banging tiny drums and blowing grass-stem flutes. The more Iktomi watched the cheerful scene and listened to the music, the more he wanted to join in. His head nodded in time to the singing and his feet itched to dance.

'Little brothers!' he called. 'Let me in! I want to join your dance!' But the mice were singing and shouting so loudly that they did not hear him.

'I shall go in anyway,' thought Iktomi and, going round to the back of the skull, he thrust his head inside.

'Look out!' shouted one of the mouse drummers. 'It is Iktomi!' And they all fled in terror.

Iktomi was now left alone and forlorn. Even worse was to come, for the buffalo skull was such a tight fit that he could not get it off. He tugged and twisted the skull and banged it on the ground until his head ached, but all to no avail.

Suddenly, he heard a low chuckle nearby and looked up. Rabbit was leaning nonchalantly against a tree, watching him.

'Rabbit!' cried Iktomi, clapping his hands. 'What a good thing you are here! I was just coming to return your shirt!' He saw Rabbit raise a disbelieving eyebrow and went on in a shocked tone, 'You surely did not think that I meant to leave you in that tree? It was just one of my jokes.'

'I suppose that you want me to help you now,' said Rabbit drily. 'Do you promise to give me back my shirt and robe if I free you from that skull?'

'Of course, Rabbit!' cried Iktomi. 'I will give you anything you want! You have only to ask.'

Rabbit picked up a large stone and brought it down on the buffalo skull with such force that he broke it in two. Iktomi fell to the ground, clutching his bruised head.

'I will have my shirt now, if you please,' said Rabbit grimly.

Iktomi looked at him slyly. Now that he was free he did not feel quite so ready to hand over Rabbit's clothes.

'Let us have a competition,' he suggested. 'Whoever shoots the greatest number of eagles, keeps both the shirt and the robe for himself!'

This time, however, Iktomi had been too clever for his own good. He had forgotten how skilled Rabbit was with his bow and arrow.

All that afternoon they shot at eagles flying overhead and every one of Rabbit's arrows found its mark. Iktomi, on the other hand, had no success at all. By the end of the day he had lost all his arrows and had not shot a single eagle. Finally, shamefaced, he conceded defeat and gave Rabbit back his shirt and robe.

Rabbit was jubilant. Taking his skin drum, he began to sing and dance in triumph. Iktomi's head still ached from being stuck inside the buffalo skull and every beat of Rabbit's drum sounded to him like a clap of thunder. With every beat he leaped higher in the air until at last he leaped right over the tree-tops and out of sight.

Of course, that was not the end of Iktomi, nor the end of his tricks. You can be sure that, wherever he went next, he continued to be a source of trouble to everyone he met.

Hasjelti's dance

In the mythology of the South-West, the first people came, not from the sky, but out of the earth. The Pueblo Indians tell how people originally lived in the darkness under the earth, unable to see or breathe. The Sun took pity on them and sent his twin sons, Watsutsi and Yanaluha, to bring them up into the daylight. The people emerged as strange creatures with horns and tails, covered in slime. Their fingers and toes were webbed and they had no mouths, but the twins cut and shaped them into the semblance of human beings with their sharp flint knives.

The twin heroes also helped to rid the world of monsters, such as the Cloud Swallower, who caused drought and famine, and the horned giant who threw people over cliffs to feed his cannibal children in the caves below.

Out of the earth there also came the Kachinas, the bringers of rain, who made the earth fertile and encouraged plants to grow. There are a great many Kachinas—animals, tribal ancestors and natural forces like wind, thunder and clouds—each with its own character and function.

At first the Kachinas themselves visited the villages with gifts of corn, skins, tools and weapons. They taught the people how to hunt and find food and how to make their clothing and pottery, but the people failed to show the Kachinas proper respect and so they came no more. However, they allowed the people to wear masks in their likenesses and to perform their dances.

Still today in Pueblo villages, Kachinas are honoured in this way. In the kiva, a ceremonial chamber often built underground, priests prepare an altar with offerings and prayer sticks, lengths of wood painted and decorated with feathers, by which messages are sent to the spirits. Then masked and costumed dancers, impersonating the Kachinas, perform sacred ceremonies to ensure a plentiful supply of rain for the growing crops.

Children are given dolls representing the Kachinas so that they can learn the myths and understand the meaning of the ceremonies.

The Holy People of the Navajo also came from the earth, driven upwards by a rising flood until they reached the present world. It was they who created the Earth Surface People, the ancestors of the

Navajo, and taught them how to live and control the forces of nature.

Foremost among the Holy People is Estanatlehi, or Changing Woman, and her husband the Sun. Their twin sons, Monster Slayer and Born for Water, are the heroes of Navajo legend. They were great warriors who destroyed most of the monsters which troubled the earth. The lava fields of the south-west are said to be the dried blood of the slain monsters. The twins did not kill them all, however, for some, like Poverty, Hunger, Old Age and Death, proved to have a place in the world and were allowed to remain.

Most of the Holy People are friendly towards human beings. Estanatlehi gave them corn and other gifts. Water Sprinkler brought rain and Spider Woman taught them to weave. Yet, because they are so powerful, the Holy People can also be dangerous, so ceremonies must be held to control threatening elements and maintain harmony with the supernatural.

Many Navajo ceremonies are concerned with curing illness, which is believed to come from the Holy People who have been offended in some way. Such ceremonies or chants, as they are called, involve songs, prayers and sometimes the making of a sandpainting depicting the Holy People. Sandpaintings are made by trickling coloured sand, cornmeal, charcoal and powdered flower petals on a plain sand floor. The patient is seated on the sandpainting and the sand applied to his body, so that good may be exchanged for evil, health for sickness.

Many myths explain how a particular chant originated and how it should be carried out. Often they tell of a hero, who through meeting some of the Holy People, acquired special power and knowledge.

In the shadow of Wind Mountain lived three brothers. Two were bold and strong, but the third, the youngest, was considered a simpleton.

While his brothers went hunting, he wandered alone all day among the rocky canyons and high mesas, through woods of juniper and pinyon or across the arid scrublands.

When the elder brothers came back to the camp in the evening, they threw down the deer, rabbits and other game which they had caught. The youngest returned only with a pine branch or a handful of feathers. He told them fantastic stories of what he had seen and heard during the day, of how he had talked with plants and animals and of how they had given him the gifts which he brought home.

This made his brothers angry. Looking up from skinning a deer or feathering an arrow, they would cry roughly, 'Hold your tongue! You do not know what you are talking about!'

In truth, they did not entirely disbelieve him, but they were jealous that he might have powers which they had not, so they constantly taunted him with being a fool and a liar.

There came a time when game grew scarce and even plants and berries were difficult to find. The brothers were reduced to gathering grass-seeds for food. They were almost always hungry.

At last, the eldest brother said, 'We cannot go on like this. We must go hunting. Somehow we will find game even if we have to travel far.' 'Let me come with you,' begged the youngest brother.
'What! You, fool?' retorted the elder. 'What use would you be, except to hinder us and frighten the game? You stay here in the camp and mind that you do not leave it until we return!'

For five days and nights the youngest brother remained alone in the camp. Each morning he scanned the horizon, but the hunters did not appear. He grew more and more anxious until finally, on the morning of the sixth day, he decided to go in search of them.
'Perhaps,' he reasoned, 'they need my help. It may be that they have killed more deer than they can carry,' and he set out in the direction they had taken.

All day he travelled without finding any trace of his brothers. As darkness fell, he stopped for the night in a cave close by a canyon. He was just settling down to sleep when he heard a great tumult overhead. Going to the mouth of the cave, he looked up and saw a flock of crows wheeling over the canyon, swooping from one cliff edge to the other. He saw fires flickering on the sides of the canyon and realized that he had stumbled by chance into the home of the Crow People.

As he watched, two crows flew down and landed near the cave. The boy drew back into the shadows and listened to what they said.

One of the crows, fluttering in great agitation, screamed, 'Somebody says . . .! Somebody says . . .!'

'What is wrong?' shouted a crow from the far side of the canyon.

'Two of our number have been slain!' replied the first crow. 'They met two hunters who had killed twelve deer. Our people followed after, hoping to join in the feast, but they grew overbold and settled on one of the carcases. One sat on the horn and the other on the backbone. The hunters drew their bows and shot them both!'

The crows on the other side of the canyon shuffled their wings and clicked their beaks. 'It is not to be wondered at!' cried one. 'Those who go after carrion in this way must expect to be killed. They died through their own stupidity and we will speak of them no more.'

In the cave, the boy sat quietly, listening to everything that was said. He knew that the hunters of whom the crows had spoken must be his brothers.

The crows gathered around their fires and began to dance, crossing back and forth over the canyon. The boy could not see them clearly but he saw their dark forms silhouetted against the firelight. He heard their songs rise into the night air, sometimes clear and bubbling like streams after rain, sometimes soft and low like the sighing of a summer breeze. All night long the songs continued and the boy listened, memorizing everything.

Towards daylight, he heard a new song begin, even sweeter and more lovely than those which had gone before, and he knew that Hasjelti must be among them — Hasjelti, the Bringer of the Dawn, who, with his brother Hostjoghon, the Twilight Bringer, made all the great songs of the world. Hasjelti's song told of the might of the sun, of the clouds over the mountains and the falling rain, of the beauty of growing plants. The boy listened entranced, straining to catch every wonderful note.

With the daylight, the music faded. The crows spread their wings and flew away towards the west. Nothing remained but the dying fires on the sides of the canyon.

The boy was filled with a great exhilaration on account of all that he had seen and heard. From what the crows had said, his brothers were not far away and he could scarcely wait to tell them his story. He continued on his way as fast as he could and soon he saw the plume of smoke rising from their campfire in the distance.

His brothers were sitting by their fire, roasting meat. They saw the boy running towards them, waving his arms excitedly.

'Here comes the fool,' said the eldest brother wearily. 'I wonder what tale he has for us now. No doubt he has seen something which no one ever saw before.'

'Let him alone,' replied the other brother. 'Perhaps strange things do happen. He cannot make them up all the time.'

When the boy reached them, the eldest brother asked, 'Well, what adventures befell you on your journey?'

The boy gasped, 'Such a night I have spent! Such singing and dancing!'

The eldest brother muttered sceptically, 'I thought it might be something like that,' but the second brother said, 'Go on. Tell us what you saw.'

'I saw the Crow People dancing all night across a canyon,' the boy replied. 'I heard them say that two hunters had killed twelve deer and then killed two of their people who tried to steal some of the meat.'

His brothers looked up in astonishment. 'How many deer did you say?' asked the eldest brother.

'Twelve,' answered the boy. 'Twelve deer.'

'And how many crows were killed?' asked the second brother.

'Two,' said the boy. 'Two crows.'

The eldest brother said slowly, 'You have told us many stories and I have never believed you, but this I must believe. We did indeed shoot twelve deer as well as two crows who came after them. I do not understand it. How do you learn these things?'

'I do not understand it either,' said the boy. 'I only know what I see and hear.'

'Well,' broke in the second brother, 'whatever the truth of the matter, it is fortunate that you came to find us. We have so much meat that we did not know how to carry it all. Now that you are here to help, we can go home.'

When they had gone half-way, they stopped to

rest on the edge of a mesa. Far below they saw four mountain sheep clambering among the rocks, stopping now and then to nibble the sparse vegetation. The eldest brother handed the boy his bow and arrows.

'You are fresher than we are,' he said. 'Go and kill one of those sheep for us.'

The boy made his way stealthily down the mesa towards the sheep and hid in a clump of sagebrush directly in their path. As the sheep approached, the boy raised his bow, but, before he could take aim, his arm stiffened and became as though dead. The sheep passed by as if oblivious of his presence.

The boy ran after them and managed to get ahead. He crouched among the stalks of a large yucca and, when the sheep came within five paces, he stood up, his bow at the ready, but for a second time his arm grew stiff and useless and the sheep passed by unharmed.

Again the boy pursued them and managed to head them off. He hid behind a small birch tree and waited.

As the sheep drew near, however, they began to change. They grew tall and slender. A shining light spread around them and they were transformed into Holy People. The first two were Hasjelti and Hostjoghon. The third was Naaskiddi, the hunchback who carries the seeds of all the plants on his shoulder and the last was Hastsezini, who brings fire and heat.

At the sight of these stately, radiant beings, the boy was stricken with terror. His weapons slipped from his hands and he fell to the ground, senseless.

The Holy People gathered around him. Hasjelti stood to the east, Hostjoghon to the south, Naaskiddi to the west and Hastsezini to the north. With their staffs they traced strange emblems in the sand around the boy's body and,

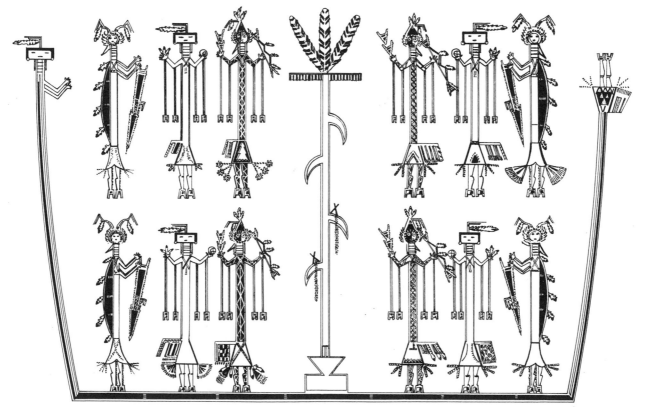

to the accompaniment of their gourd rattles, they sang songs to aid his recovery.

At last the boy opened his eyes. All that had happened came back to him and he sat up, looking round in awe and wonder. The Holy People had once more assumed the form of mountain sheep.

'Why did you seek to kill us?' asked one. 'Do you not see that you are one of us?' The boy looked down and saw that he too had become a mountain sheep.

'Do not be alarmed,' continued the sheep. 'We mean you no harm. There is to be a dance far off beyond the mountains to the north. We want you to come with us. We will dress you as we dress and teach you to dance.'

The boy's brothers were watching from the top of the mesa. They could not understand what was going on. They saw the boy lying on the ground, but the Holy People were invisible to them. 'Something is wrong,' said one. 'We had better go down and find out what has happened to the boy.'

They scrambled hastily down the rocky face of the mesa, but by the time they reached its foot, their brother had gone. They found the place where he had lain and the strange designs in the sand, and they saw, disappearing into the distance, five mountain sheep.

They chased after them and tried to head them off, but without success. The sheep evaded their every move and vanished among the rocks. Sadly the hunters turned homewards.
'For so long we would not believe him,' said one bitterly. 'Our brother told us many things and we would not listen. Now he has gone with the sheep and we may never see him again.'

The sheep travelled far into the northern mountains and beyond, until, at dusk, they reached a great open space over which arched the protective body of Nattsilit, the Rainbow Woman. Many of the Holy People were gathered there and the boy's eyes were dazzled by the shining splendour of their presence.

Yet none was more handsome than Hasjelti, who once more had thrown off the guise of a mountain sheep. In his hair he wore an eagle tail, each plume tipped with soft down. His shirt was of finest cotton and his fringed leggings of white buckskin. Turquoises hung from his ears and his head was bathed in red sunlight.

With the arrival of the song-makers, the fires were lit and the dance began. All through the night the boy watched the chanting dancers, weaving, stamping and swaying in the firelight. Hasjelti, the leader of the dance, instructed him in all their movements and taught him all their songs. He told him of the ceremonies which the Earth Surface people should perform in preparation for the dance and of the deerskin masks which they should wear when they wished to impersonate the Holy People. He also taught him to make paintings depicting the Holy People in the colours of earth and flowers. The boy listened and remembered everything.

At last, as the night gave way to day, Hasjelti plucked two ears of corn from a tall plant growing nearby. He gave them to the boy, placing one in each hand, and said, 'We will keep you with us no longer. You have learned everything. Go now and tell your people and teach them to do as we do.'

A great weariness swept over the boy and he closed his eyes. When he opened them again, he found himself at the foot of the mesa where he had first encountered the mountain sheep. He was completely alone, but, in each hand, he held an ear of corn.

When he reached home, his brothers welcomed him with open arms. No longer was he despised as a liar and a fool. Everyone was eager to listen to his story and people came from miles around to see and hear the boy who had been with the Holy People.

The boy taught the people all the songs and dances as Hasjelti had instructed them and he showed them how to make sandpaintings and masks to represent the Holy People. Through the special knowledge which he had been given, he was able to cure sickness and disease and so won great love and respect.

All this happened a long time ago, but the ceremonies, songs and dances which the boy learned from the Holy People have never been forgotten. Still, when the Navajo wish to drive away evil and bring health and well-being in its place, they perform the chant called Hasjelti Dailjis — Hasjelti's Dance.

The Corn Maidens

To the Pueblo Indians corn was not only an important food crop. It had a sacred power all of its own. A perfect ear of corn, fully kernelled, was the emblem of a priest or ceremonial leader and, wrapped in beads and feathers, was the chief offering laid on an altar. Cornmeal was used to anoint priests and sacred objects, and to make a pathway to and from the kiva. It was sprinkled to bless fields and houses and to protect newborn children.

In the beginning only grass grew on the earth and the first people gathered the seeds for food, but it was a meagre diet and they prayed to the Sun to send them something more. They made offerings of the largest, most brightly coloured grass-seeds they could find and they built a great fire in his honour. The Sun heard their pleas for help and sent from the Seed People six sisters, the beautiful Corn Maidens.

In their white cloaks, embroidered with all the colours of the rainbow, the sisters danced among the grasses in the firelight and, as they danced, the plants grew tall and strong, with long feathery leaves and tasselled stems. With gentle fingers, the Corn Maidens touched one of the plants and the fire burned with a yellow flame. They touched another and the fire took hold, billowing clouds of blue smoke into the air. They caressed a third and the fire glowed, hot and red. As they came to the fourth, the flames reached the height of their power, burning with a clear white light. With the fifth plant, the fire threw up many-coloured sparks and, with the sixth, it died down, leaving only blackened ashes. Thus came the six colours of corn known to the Pueblos — yellow, blue, red, white, speckled and black.

The Corn Maidens remained among the first people for a long time, honoured and loved for the goodness which they had brought. The people knew that when the Corn Maidens danced in their fields, the corn would grow strong and healthy and, with the help of the Sun and the Uwanami, the Rain Makers, would ripen into a rich and fruitful harvest.

There came a time, however, when the people grew slovenly and forgetful of the debt which they owed to the Corn Maidens. No longer did they reap the corn with patient care and stack it neatly in their storerooms. Instead, they tore the ears roughly from the stems and threw them down on dirty, unswept floors, trampling them heedlessly underfoot. They allowed the bright kernels to rot where they lay or fed them to their animals. They ground far more corn than they could use and threw the surplus away or used it to stuff skin bags for their ball games.

The Corn Maidens were hurt and saddened by this careless treatment of their gifts, but the people paid no heed to their chidings, turning away from them with coldness and disdain.

At last, the oldest Maiden, Yellow Corn, called her sisters together and said, 'It is time for us to leave this place, for the people no longer respect us as they once did. Let us go far away so that in time they will learn how much they need us.'

Drawing their white cloaks around them, the Corn Maidens stole silently away in the heavy mists of early morning. They took the road to the south, Yellow Corn leading them and Black Corn following last to darken the road so that none should see where they had gone.

Their journey led them to the Kachina Village where Pautiwa, chief of the Kachinas, welcomed them. The Maidens told him how they had been abused and neglected and, as he listened, Pautiwa grew grave and thoughtful.
'It is not good that you should leave the people forever,' he declared. 'Yet truly they deserve to be punished for their foolishness. Come with me. I will hide you until they learn the error of their ways.'

Pautiwa led them to the shores of a lake. He changed into a large, snow-white duck and, gathering the Corn Maidens under his wings, sank into the water.

At first, the people did not care that the Maidens had left them, for now that corn was plentiful, they thought that they had no further need of them. They continued to squander their stocks of corn and when planting time came, very little seed remained in their storerooms.

They prepared their fields and planted the seeds as usual, but, although the sun shone and the rain fell, the corn did not flourish. The few ears gathered were small and pale, the kernels wizened and hard.

Year by year, the stock of seed corn diminished. The people sowed what little they had, but frost and drought withered the sickly young plants.

At last the storerooms were empty and the people were starving. They searched the darkest corners of their houses for any kernels which might have been overlooked, seizing upon even those which were dry and shrivelled which, in the days of plenty, they would have tossed aside in disgust. Once more they were reduced to eating wild seeds and cactus stems, but soon even this unpalatable food grew scarce.

The bow-priests, those who led the people in war and protected the village, called a council. 'Our foolish pride has driven away the corn,' they said. 'Now our people are dying of hunger. We must find the Corn Maidens and beg them to return. But who can tell us where they have gone?'

They sought out Eagle and told him of the lost Corn Maidens. The great bird replied, 'Your troubles are at an end. I will find the Maidens before the day is over, for nothing escapes my keen eye.'

Eagle flew far into the clouds. He circled north, west, south and east, high over mountain ridges and pine forests, scanning the earth.

In the evening he returned. The people heard the beat of his wings and rushed eagerly to meet him but, in spite of his confident promise, he brought no news. He had found no trace of the Corn Maidens.
'They must indeed be well hidden,' he said, 'for I flew in all directions, yet could not find them anywhere. Send for my younger brother, Falcon. He is not as strong as I am and flies closer to the ground. Perhaps he can help you.'
'Eagle failed, did he?' laughed Falcon, when the bow-priests told him of their quest. 'Little wonder! He soars above the clouds, yet thinks that he can see under every bush and into every shadow. You should have come to me first, for not so much as a sparrow or a mouse can hide from me!'

Falcon flew low over the earth, skimming the tops of trees and bushes and swooping into every cranny in the rocks. Yet, in the end, he was no more successful than Eagle had been.
'Your Corn Maidens are nowhere to be found!' he cried as he flew away. 'They must be lost forever!'

As a last resort, the bow-priests turned to Raven. Bright-eyed, he listened to what they had

to say. Then he threw back his head and burst into mocking laughter.

'Do you think,' he cried rudely, 'that you can find the Corn Maidens by searching the mountain tops and bushes? Do you not know whose music calls the Maidens into the fields, whose breath draws the plants from the earth? Seek out Paiyatuma, you dolts!' He flapped his wings in their faces and flew away, cackling.

The bow-priests looked at one another. 'Paiyatuma!' they cried. 'Of course!'

Paiyatuma it was who brought the dawn and scattered his bright beads of dew to freshen the earth and make it green. His home was in a rocky cavern on the banks of a stream and, even as they approached, the bow-priests heard the sound of his music above the rushing waters. The mouth of the cavern was wreathed in mists and a rainbow arched overhead. Inside sat Paiyatuma, playing his flute. He wore a crown of flowers and around him fluttered myriads of bright butterflies, drawn there by his playing.

'Help us, Paiyatuma, Bringer of Dawn!' begged the bow-priests. 'Our Corn Maidens have fled from us and taken the corn with them. If you cannot discover their hiding-place, there is no hope for us!'

Paiyatuma smiled. 'Return to your homes,' he said. 'The Corn Maidens cannot resist my music. I will find them wherever they are and bring them back to you.'

Paiyatuma prepared four prayer sticks. He painted each one a different colour—yellow, blue, white, red—and decorated them with eagle down. Turning to the east, he planted the yellow stick upright in the ground. The eagle down fluttered for a moment, then hung still. Paiyatuma turned to the north with the white stick and to the west with the blue and the same thing happened. Finally he set the red stick to the south. The eagle down fluttered as before, but, instead of ceasing its movement, it began to sway gently and steadily, to and fro, northward and southward.

'Ah!' said Paiyatuma softly. 'Then southward shall I go, for it is there that the Corn Maidens are hidden. It is their breath that so moves the eagle down!'

Placing his flute to his lips, Paiyatuma set out towards the south. As he went, the flowers unfolded their petals and all the butterflies of the world danced overhead. His music filled the air and reached the lake where the Corn Maidens lay sleeping, cradled in Pautiwa's soft white feathers. They stirred and awoke. Pautiwa carried them to the edge of the lake and, raising his wings, set them on the shore.

Paiyatuma came towards them and called out, 'I have come to take you home. The people need you. They have learned a bitter lesson and beg your forgiveness.'

The Maidens turned to their protector Pautiwa. He had thrown off his feathered disguise and now stood before them, stately and resplendent in richly embroidered robes of white cotton. 'Yes, my children,' he said. 'Now it is time for you to return. We will go together.'

With Paiyatuma leading them, the Corn Maidens returned to where the people waited, half in hope, half in despair. Pautiwa followed, carrying a basket of cornmeal and a gourd filled with water which he had scooped from the lake.

The procession entered the house which the bow-priests had specially prepared. Pautiwa scattered cornmeal from his basket to bless the house and laid his gourd before the altar, saying, 'I bring you this sacred water so that, when you plant your corn, the rain will always come to give you a good harvest.'

Then Paiyatuma raised his flute to his lips once more and all day long the Corn Maidens danced through the village. The people wept with joy to see them again.

As night fell, the music died away and the dancing ceased. The Corn Maidens, one after the other, placed on the ground a tray of seed corn, each of her own colour. Then they slipped away into the gathering shadows.

Now Paiyatuma stepped forward and laid his flute alongside the trays. 'I shall come no more amongst you,' he said, 'but I leave you my flute and the secret of its playing so that you will always be able to make music for the dancing of the Corn Maidens.' With those words, he too vanished into the darkness.

Only Pautiwa now remained among the people. He saw them look anxiously around for the Corn Maidens and said kindly, 'Have no fear. The Maidens have not fled away as before, but neither they nor I will be seen by you again. Henceforth, you will choose from amongst yourselves those to represent us and, in this way, the Corn Maidens will come once more to bless the seed corn and instruct you in its care.'

All through the night, Pautiwa sat among the people, teaching them the ceremonies, songs and dances of the Corn Maidens. They listened eagerly, promising that, ever afterwards, they would keep the customs of the Maidens and cherish their gifts.

With the coming of day, Pautiwa arose and said, 'Do all as I have told you and with the changing seasons your corn will grow and the seed will be renewed.' Then he faded away into the morning mists and was seen no more.

Rabbit shoots the sun

It was the height of summer, the time of year called Hadotso, the Great Heat. All day long, from a blue and cloudless sky, the blazing sun beat down upon the earth. No rain had fallen for many days and there was not the slightest breath of wind to cool the stifling air. Everything was hot and dry. Even the rose-red cliffs of the canyons and mesas seemed to take on a more brilliant colour than before.

The animals drooped with misery. They were parched and hungry, for it was too hot to hunt for food and, panting heavily, they sought what shade they could under the rocks and bushes.

Rabbit was the unhappiest of all. Twice that day the shimmering heat had tempted him across the baked earth towards visions of water and cool, shady trees. He had exhausted himself in his desperate attempts to reach them, only to find the mirages dissolve before him, receding further and further into the distance.

Now, tired and wretched, he dragged himself into the shadow of an overhanging rock and crouched there listlessly. His soft fur was caked with the red dust of the desert. His head swam and his eyes ached from the sun's glare.
'Why does it have to be so hot?' he groaned. 'What have we done to deserve such torment?' He squinted up at the sun and shouted furiously, 'Go away! You are making everything too hot!'

Sun took no notice at all and continued to pour down his fiery beams, forcing Rabbit to retreat once more into the shade of the rock. 'Sun needs to be taught a lesson,' grumbled Rabbit. 'I have a good mind to go and fight him. If he refuses to stop shining, I will kill him!'

His determination to punish Sun made him forget his weariness and, in spite of the oppressive heat, he set off at a run towards the eastern edge of the world where the Sun came up each morning.

As he ran, he practised with his bow and arrows and, to make himself brave and strong, he fought with everything which crossed his path. He fought with the gophers and the lizards. He hurled his throwing stick at beetles, ants and dragonflies. He shot at the yucca and the giant cactus. He became a very fierce rabbit indeed.

By the time he reached the edge of the world, Sun had left the sky and was nowhere to be seen.
'The coward!' sneered Rabbit. 'He is afraid to fight, but he will not

escape me so easily,' and he settled to wait behind a clump of bushes.

In those days, Sun did not appear slowly as he does now. Instead he rushed up over the horizon and into the heavens with one mighty bound. Rabbit knew that he would have to act quickly in order to ambush him and he fixed his eyes intently on the spot where the Sun usually appeared.

Sun, however, had heard all Rabbit's threats and had watched him fighting. He knew that he was lying in wait among the bushes. He was not at all afraid of this puny creature and he thought that he might have some amusement at his expense.

He rolled some distance away from his usual place and swept up into the sky before Rabbit knew what was happening. By the time Rabbit had gathered his startled wits and released his bowstring, Sun was already high above him and out of range.

Rabbit stamped and shouted with rage and vexation. Sun laughed and laughed and shone even more fiercely than before.

Although almost dead from heat, Rabbit would not give up. Next morning he tried again, but this time Sun came up in a different place and evaded him once more.

Day after day the same thing happened. Sometimes Sun sprang up on Rabbit's right, sometimes on his left and sometimes straight in front of him, but always where Rabbit least expected him.

One morning, however, Sun grew careless. He rose more leisurely than usual and, this time, Rabbit was ready. Swiftly he drew his bow. His arrow whizzed through the air and buried itself deep in Sun's side.

Rabbit was jubilant! At last he had shot his enemy! Wild with joy, he leaped up and down. He rolled on the ground, hugging himself. He turned somersaults. He looked at Sun again — and stopped short.

Where his arrow had pierced Sun, there was a gaping wound and, from that wound, there gushed a stream of liquid fire. Suddenly it seemed as if the whole world had been set ablaze. Flames shot up and rushed towards Rabbit, crackling and roaring.

Rabbit paused not a moment longer. He took to his heels in panic and ran as fast as he could

away from the fire. He spied a lone cottonwood tree and scuttled towards it.
'Everything is burning!' he cried. 'Will you shelter me?'

The cottonwood shook its slender branches mournfully. 'What can I do?' it asked. 'I will be burned to the ground.'

Rabbit ran on. Behind him, the flames were coming closer. He could feel their breath on his back. A greasewood tree lay in his path.
'Hide me! Hide me!' Rabbit gasped. 'The fire is coming.'
'I cannot help you,' answered the greasewood tree. 'I will be burned up roots and branches.'

Terrified and almost out of breath, Rabbit continued to run, but his strength was failing. He could feel the fire licking at his heels and his fur was beginning to singe. Suddenly he heard a voice calling to him.
'Quickly, come under me! The fire will pass over me so swiftly that it will only scorch my top.'

It was the voice of a small green bush with flowers like bunches of cotton capping its thin branches. Gratefully, Rabbit dived below it and lay there quivering, his eyes tightly shut, his ears flat against his body.

With a thunderous roar, the sheet of flame leaped overhead. The little bush crackled and sizzled. Then, gradually, the noise receded and everything grew quiet once more.

Rabbit raised his head cautiously and looked around. Everywhere the earth lay black and smoking, but the fire had passed on. He was safe!

The little bush which had sheltered him was no longer green. Burned and scorched by the fire, it had turned a golden yellow. People now call it the desert yellow brush, for, although it first grows green, it always turns yellow when it feels the heat of the sun.

Rabbit never recovered from his fright. To this day, he bears brown spots where the fire scorched the back of his neck. He is no longer fierce and quarrelsome, but runs and hides at the slightest noise.

As for Sun, he too was never quite the same. He now makes himself so bright that no one can look at him long enough to sight an arrow and he always peers very warily over the horizon before he brings his full body into view.

The theft of fire

The Indians of the Western Desert had little time or opportunity for elaborate ceremonies. Those which they did hold were principally concerned with the never-ending quest for food. In summer, for example, they danced to honour the birds and animals and, when communal antelope hunts were arranged, shamans chanted special songs to call the wandering herds.

In the coastal strip between the Sierras and the Pacific Ocean more colourful spectacles were staged. Among many of the tribes there were secret societies which, throughout the winter months, organized cycles of ceremonies in which dancers, decked with paint, feathers and grass, portrayed supernatural beings, rather as the Pueblo Indians impersonated the Kachinas. Among the Pomo Indians, the chief spirits were represented by dancers who wore special head-dresses of eagle or buzzard feathers and whose bodies were painted black or draped with black feather capes. The dances were intended to bring rain and to ward off such disasters as sickness, flood or earthquake.

It was after a death that the most impressive ceremonies were performed. According to some of the coastal tribes, the souls of the dead lived on an island far across the sea, but others believed that they went to the Sky Land by the path of the sun or on the Milky Way. Ghosts were much feared and, when someone died, his body was buried or cremated with all possible ceremony in order to placate his spirit. Mourning ceremonies were held annually to honour the dead with offerings and songs which told how Eagle, one of the first people, flew all over the world seeking to escape death, but found it everywhere.

It was generally believed that the earth and sky had always existed, although not in their present form, for they had to be modified to suit the needs of mankind. This was done by two brothers. One, the elder of the two, made things pleasant and happy, but the other introduced suffering and hardship into what might otherwise have been a perfect world.

In the desert area the good brother was usually associated with an animal spirit such as Eagle, Puma or Wolf. In California he was a rather more remote being. To the Yuki he was Taikomol, He Who Walks Alone, to the Cahto, Nagaicho, the Great Traveller, to the Wintun

Olelbis, He Who Sits Above and to the Maidu, Kodoyanpe, the Earth Namer.

The younger brother is always Coyote, who is the most prominent character in the mythology of this area, constantly meddling and causing trouble. A Maidu myth tells how life was very easy to begin with. At night the women set their baskets by the doors of their huts and in the morning found them overflowing with food. Coyote, however, put a stop to this practice, declaring that it would make people lazy, so now women must work hard to fill their baskets.

According to the Ute, Wolf originally wanted people to have more than one death, but Coyote disagreed, saying that, when someone died, that should be the end. Coyote won the argument and a single death became the rule but, as so often happened, Coyote's scheme worked to his own disadvantage and caused him great misery. His own son died and, when he asked Wolf to change the rule, Wolf refused, reminding him that it was Coyote himself who had insisted on death being final.

Other Coyote stories explain how animals achieved their present forms. Bear, for example, had a long tail until Coyote persuaded him that he could catch fish by dangling it in a stream. The water was so cold that Bear's tail was frozen off and so has been short ever since.

On the other hand, as the following story shows, Coyote did sometimes perform good and useful deeds.

Long ago the Indians had no fire. Naturally, this made life rather difficult. In order to prepare their food, they had to collect stones warmed by the sun and use those for heating water and for cooking. In winter the only way in which they could keep warm was to wrap themselves in rabbitskin blankets and huddle together. It was all extremely unsatisfactory.

One day, as Coyote was out hunting, something floated through the air and landed close beside him. It was a small piece of charred reed, no longer than a man's finger. Coyote picked it up and turned it over in his paw, examining it closely. He could see that it was a reed, but he could not understand what had happened to make it appear so blackened and dry. 'This is most strange,' he said to himself. 'Where

can it have come from? What has changed it so?'

He carried it back to his village and showed everyone what he had found, but nobody could explain the mystery. He summoned a council of all the birds, sure that one of them must know the answer, but none, not even those who flew highest and furthest, had seen anything like it or knew from where it could have come.

After long deliberation, Coyote said, 'It seems to me that this reed has been subjected to a great heat, greater even than that of the sun. It was carried here by the western wind. Therefore, somewhere to the west, there is fire. We must find it and bring it back. We will go in search of it tomorrow.'

That night, while everyone was asleep, Coyote prowled restlessly about his hut, turning the matter over in his mind and formulating a plan. He felt sure that he was on the verge of a great discovery and he could hardly wait for morning to arrive.

At first light, just as the village was stirring, Coyote hurried down to the river and collected a bundle of reeds. He spread them out on the ground and began to beat them with a heavy stick, crushing them into fine shreds. Then he rubbed black paint into the shredded mass until it resembled tangled human hair. Finally, he brushed it smooth and put it on his head like a wig, the long strands reaching to the ground and covering his feet.

Everyone watched in amazement, wondering what he could be up to, but Coyote kept his plan to himself, for he was a secretive animal and did not like to give too much away. That was how he managed to retain his power among the people.

When all the birds were ready for the journey, Coyote led them out of the village, his reed wig rolled into a bundle and tied securely to his tail.

For several days they travelled westwards, camping overnight in caves or under bushes. Each day Coyote sent a scout ahead to spy out the land, first Eagle, then Hawk, Crow and Owl, but none of them found any trace of fire. It began to look as if their journey might prove fruitless. Some of the smaller birds were tired and spoke of turning back, but Coyote said, 'Let us go on a little further. Remember the burned reed. It must have come from somewhere.'

Finally it was Hummingbird's turn to go. Although he was such a tiny bird, he flew with the speed of lightning and vanished swiftly into the distance. He was gone for a very long time, much longer than any of the others, but at last, just as they were setting up camp for the night, he returned—and he brought news!

Hovering in front of Coyote, he shrilled, 'I have not managed to find fire itself, but far in the distance, just where the earth and sky come together, there I thought the ground looked a little smoky!' Coyote's eyes gleamed with excitement. Perhaps fire was not so far off after all!

Next day, the travellers scaled a high mountain and stopped on its peak to look around. To the west lay several mountain ranges, their tops shrouded in haze. Once more Hummingbird was sent to explore and, when he returned, he was so excited that he could barely speak.

'Beyond three mountains,' he gasped, 'I came to another as black as night and standing all alone. On its flat top I saw a village and in the centre of the village I saw something bright and shining which moved constantly, yet never stirred from the spot. And the air above it was misty blue!'

'There!' cried Coyote triumphantly. 'What did I tell you? I knew we were going in the right direction! That must be the source of fire!'

A tremendous hubbub broke out among the birds as they all congratulated each other on the success of their venture.

'Wait! Wait!' shouted Coyote above the din. 'We do not yet have fire! Now listen closely,' he went on, as the clamour died down, 'you may be sure that the owners of the fire guard it jealously and will try to keep it from us. When we reach the village, I will persuade the people to hold a dance. During the dance I will whoop twice. At the first whoop, you must draw apart from the dancers and, at the second, you must fly as fast as you can back in the direction we have come. Do not hesitate for an instant or all will be lost.'

They set out again, travelling speedily, until at last they reached the mountain of which Hummingbird had spoken. It was black, as he had said, for it was made of obsidian and its sheer, smooth sides glittered in the sun.

At the top they found a band of warriors waiting, sullen and aggressive, their weapons held ready. Their chief stepped forward. He wore a tall crown of blue and yellow feathers. His leggings and moccasins were of black buckskin and his shirt was painted a glowing fiery red. 'What has brought strangers like you to the Fire Mountain?' he asked harshly. 'Do you come in peace or to take away that which is ours?'

Coyote said humbly, 'We mean no harm.' He indicated his companions. 'How could we, poor creatures as we are? As we were passing this way, we thought we might take the opportunity to visit you and perhaps see your dancing, of which we have heard so much.'

The chief smiled and his warriors relaxed. 'It is true,' he nodded, 'that we hold many fine dances here. Since you come in friendship, we will hold one tonight in your honour. Come, join us round our fire.'

Coyote and the birds gazed wide-eyed at the marvellous fire. They had never seen anything like it. Its heart glowed red and the flames danced as if alive, blue and yellow, while the smoke billowed into the air.

At the chief's command, preparations were made for the coming festivities. A splendid feast was set out and the great fire built up even higher. Everyone got ready for the dance, decorating themselves in all their finery.

Coyote untied the reed wig from his tail and shook it out straight and smooth. Placing it on his head, he parted it in the middle and plaited it so that it hung over his shoulders in two thick, heavy braids. The Fire People thought that this must be his special dancing costume and they admired it greatly.

The dance began and continued all through the night. Coyote was the most exuberant and tireless dancer of them all. As the first signs of day streaked the eastern sky and still he danced, the puzzled birds looked at one another, wondering if perhaps he had forgotten the purpose of their visit to the Fire Village.

Suddenly, without warning, Coyote let out a high-pitched whoop. The Fire People looked at him, startled, and faltered in their dancing. 'Oh forgive me!' cried Coyote. 'It is just my way of showing appreciation. I cannot recall when I enjoyed myself more, nor indeed,' he added archly, looking about him, 'when I last saw so many beautiful girls!'

The Fire Women giggled and hid their faces coyly, flattered by his compliments. The chief laughed approvingly and the dance went on.

Coyote glanced round surreptitiously and saw that, in accordance with his instructions, the birds had withdrawn from the circle of dancers and were huddled on the sidelines, awaiting his next move.

The day grew lighter and the stars faded. Smoothing his reed braids, Coyote danced closer to the fire. It was burning low now. Only a few flames still flickered among the embers. Coyote circled it once, twice, then he whooped again. With one swift movement, he tore off his head-dress and dashed it into the fire.

Sparks caught the dry reeds instantly. Tongues of flame shot up and crackled into a blaze. As soon as he was sure that the reeds were well alight, Coyote seized the bundle in his teeth and ran as fast as he could out of the Fire Village, slithering down the black mountainside to the valley below.

The birds had flown at his signal and were already waiting there, excited and noisy. Coyote tossed the blazing bundle of reeds to Eagle who caught it expertly in his powerful talons. 'Fly! Fly!' shouted Coyote. 'Fly, all of you, as you have never flown before!' And, with the birds streaming above him, he raced at full speed towards the mountains which they had crossed the previous day.

Back in the Fire Village, all was confusion. The Fire People were panic-stricken for not only had Coyote taken fire away with him, he had put their own fire out. Nothing remained but a smouldering heap of blackened cinders. 'We have been tricked!' roared the chief. 'After them at once! We must get our fire back, for without it we have no power at all!'

Looking back, Coyote saw the Fire People pouring down the mountain. Their war-cries

117

echoed behind him and their arrows whistled overhead. The chase had begun!

Over the mountains sped Coyote and the birds, across the plains, through valleys and ravines, the avenging Fire People hard on their heels. The birds took turns in carrying the torch. As each one began to flag, he passed it to another before flying away to find a safe hiding-place in which to rest and recover his strength.

Finally, only Coyote and Hummingbird remained. The little bird bore the torch bravely, but he was very tired and Coyote saw that it was now his turn.

'Give me the fire!' he called. 'I will carry it back to our village.'

Hummingbird dropped the torch at his feet and darted away out of sight. The bundle of reeds was still burning brightly. Coyote quickly lashed it to his tail and set off alone.

Behind him, the Fire People were growing more and more angry, for Coyote still ran swiftly and they were no nearer to recovering their fire. 'Well,' snarled the chief to his men, 'if we cannot have our fire, then no one else will have it either! I will see to that!'

He called on his friends, the Thunder Man and the Cloud People, to send down a violent storm to douse the fire once and forever.

The thunder crashed and the rain poured down in torrents. It streamed down the mountains and filled the valleys. Coyote was drenched, his fur matted and plastered to his body. He floundered on through the flood-water, holding his tail erect to keep the torch dry.

He looked back and saw, to his horror, that his pursuers were gaining on him. To make matters worse, the fire was going out! Only a few sparks now glimmered among the reeds and, even as he looked, they began to dim. Had it all been in vain?

In desperation, Coyote looked about him and saw a small cave high in the rocks above. He dragged himself up towards it and threw himself inside. With his last ounce of strength, he rolled a huge boulder across the entrance, sealing it against the Fire People. He untied the bundle of reeds from his tail and his heart sank. The fire seemed completely dead. He bent over it and blew, but nothing happened. He blew again, harder, and in the middle of the bundle

something glowed faintly, then more brightly.

Luckily the cave was dry and full of brushwood. Coyote threw some wisps of sagebrush over the reeds, fanning and blowing with all his might, until at last a little flame sprang up, then another, and another. He heaped sticks into the flames and soon the fire blazed up once more. Coyote sank back with a sigh of relief, his damp fur steaming in the heat.

The Fire People had now given up the chase, for they were sure that the rainstorm must have extinguished the fire completely.
'We may as well go home,' growled the chief. 'Yet I will make quite certain that the thief does not escape!' He called once more on his friends to send a snowstorm and an icy wind to freeze Coyote to death.

The snow fell heavily and the flood-water turned to thick ice, but, in his cave, Coyote was warm and dry. He curled up comfortably and, worn out by his exertions, fell fast asleep.

When he awoke, he was relieved to find the fire still burning cheerfully. He peered cautiously out of the cave. Ice and snow lay everywhere, but the Fire People had gone.

With their departure, a soft south wind sprang up and the ice began to melt. The warm sun came out and the flood-waters retreated.

Coyote hollowed out a length of sagebrush and packed the tube with glowing embers from the fire. He sealed it up and tied it to his tail before starting out for home once more.

When he arrived at the village, the people were cooking their evening meal. 'Throw away those heated stones!' shouted Coyote. 'We do not need them any more, for now we have fire!'

He laid the sagebrush tube on a bed of soft, dry grass and drilled into it with a piece of hard greasewood whittled to a fine point. Sparks flew from the tube, setting the grass alight. The people gasped in wonder to see how quickly and easily fire came.

Soon all the birds who had stopped to rest began to return. Coyote gave each one a burning twig and sent them to carry fire all over the world.

Now, thanks to Coyote, everyone has fire. His descendants remember his exploit with pride and, to this day, all have a dark tip to their tails where the fire scorched Coyote's tail as he carried it.

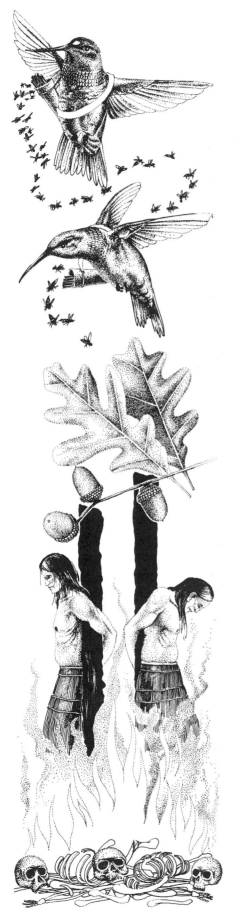

The Hummingbird brothers

Many stories of the Far West, like those told in other parts of North America, depict the first inhabitants of the world as wise and powerful animals, with many human attributes and habits. The Pomo Indians referred to these first beings as the Bird People, even although they included animals, reptiles and insects as well as birds.

In a village on the shores of Clear Lake lived three Bird People—two young Hummingbird boys and their grandmother Turtle Woman. The boys were puzzled by the great number of empty houses in the village. Although many were now falling into ruin, they still contained furnishings, with tools and baskets lying on the floors, as if the occupants had left hurriedly, meaning to return before long. Each time they asked their grandmother what had happened, she looked sad and tried to change the subject, but at last, under their persistent questioning, she agreed to tell them the story.

'Once,' began Turtle Woman, brushing away a tear, 'there were many people living here. Falcon was our chief and we were very happy. Roots, seeds and berries grew in abundance, the lake was well stocked with fish and herds of deer roamed the hills. One year, however, there was a terrible drought. No rain fell at all and everything withered. The streams dried up and the deer moved away in search of food. Our acorn harvest, on which we depended so much, was a disaster. Falcon sent out messengers to seek fresh supplies and eventually Blue Jay brought news of a small crop of acorns somewhere to the east. Then Falcon said that we must go and collect this crop and bring it back to our village. Everyone went, men, women and children, carrying baskets to bring back the acorns. You were left behind because you were still babies, too small for the journey, and I stayed to take care of you. Our people did not expect to be gone long, a week or two at most, but,' and here fresh tears welled up in Turtle Woman's eyes, 'they never returned. From that day to this, not one of them has ever been seen again and I am afraid that something dreadful must have happened to them all!' She broke down, sobbing as if her heart would break.

'Do not distress yourself, Grandmother,' the boys comforted her. 'We will go east in search of our people and, if any are still alive, we will bring them back.'

'Oh no!' cried Turtle Woman. 'I have heard that in the east is the Sun

Village, where the people are cannibals. If you go there, you will be killed!'

The Hummingbird brothers reassured her, saying stoutly, 'We have bows and arrows and we know well how to use them. We will return, never fear!'

The boys passed through several villages on their journey eastwards. Many of the inhabitants remembered the Bird People passing through in search of acorns several years before, but none knew where they had gone or what had happened to them.

After several days' travel, the brothers came to the village where Buzzard was chief. They told him the purpose of their journey and he answered grimly, 'You would be better to turn back. There are many dangers over there in the east.'

'We must find our people,' replied the elder brother firmly. 'We must go on.'

'Well,' said the Buzzard, 'you do not have much further to go. Do you see that mountain over there? Beyond it lies the Sun Village. That is the place you are looking for. That is where your people are held captive.'

That evening the boys camped under a tree at the foot of the mountain. In the morning a loud, angry buzzing awakened them and, looking up, they saw that a swarm of yellow-jacket hornets had built their nest in the tree above them. Hastily the boys lit a fire under the tree. The smoke quietened the hornets, making them slow and drowsy.

'These insects seem very dangerous when angry,' said one of the boys thoughtfully. 'Let us take them with us. They may prove useful if we are attacked,' and they scooped the stupefied yellowjackets into their quivers.

When they reached the top of the mountain, they saw the Sun Village spread out on the plain below. The houses gleamed white in the sun for they were built from the bleached bones of those whom the Sun People had killed and eaten.

The brothers made their way stealthily down the mountainside and soon reached the outskirts of the village. They sheltered behind a large mound of acorns to see what was going on.

Suddenly a woman appeared round the side of the mound, a basket in her hand to collect acorns. She started back in alarm when she saw the strangers. Then she looked at them curiously. 'Are you not Bird People?' she asked. 'What brings you to this terrible place?'

The boys told their story and joy and amazement dawned in the woman's face. 'I am your mother!' she cried. 'I have often wept for my babies who were left behind when we went to gather acorns. I never thought that I would see you again!'

She told them how she and her companions had been attacked by the Sun People and how many of the Bird People had been killed in the fighting. The others had been taken prisoner and were now slaves in the Sun Village.

'You too will be killed if you remain here!' she added in horror. 'Go now, before you are discovered.'

'No!' declared the boys. 'We will ask the Sun chief to release you and, if he refuses, we will find some way of forcing him to do so!'

The boys would not be dissuaded from their purpose and, in spite of their mother's pleas, they marched resolutely through the village, right into the Sun chief's house.

Datca, the Sun Man, was enormously fat and ugly. He had a huge mouth and throat which enabled him to swallow people whole. His head was completely bald and hard, stiff whiskers covered his face. Once he had been very powerful and had worn the sun round his neck, keeping the rest of the world in darkness, but Coyote had stolen the sun and placed it in the sky to shine over everything. This blow to his power had done nothing to improve Datca's temper and he was now even more savage and cruel than he had been before.

When the boys entered, he glared at them with his great fierce eyes and, without giving them a chance to speak, roared to his men, 'Seize them!

Take them away! Tie them to the stakes!'

Before they could escape, the brothers found themselves lashed to two poles which stood in front of the fire. Datca ordered the fire to be built up, for he meant to roast the boys alive.

The flames leaped up almost to the ceiling, giving off a tremendous heat. The boys struggled to free themselves from their bonds, but they were tied too securely and, overcome by the heat, they fainted.

When the Sun People saw their bodies become limp and their heads loll on their shoulders, they thought exultantly that they had killed them. They too had become very hot from the fire and so, leaving the boys still tied to the stakes, they went down to the river to bathe.

As soon as they were gone, the boys' mother slipped in and swiftly untied the ropes which held them. She dashed cold water over their faces and the boys began to revive.

As soon as they had fully recovered, they strolled down to the river as though nothing untoward had happened and plunged in among the astonished Sun People.

The Sun Man looked at them furiously. 'What kind of people are these?' he muttered. 'I thought that I had killed them, yet they are still alive!'

However, to the brothers he said, 'I merely wished to test your courage and endurance, my friends. You have borne yourselves well, and we would be honoured if you would join us in hunting rabbits in the woods yonder.'

The Hummingbird brothers were not at all deceived by his unctuous words, but they agreed to join the hunters. Their mother ran after them and, under the pretext of offering them food, whispered urgently, 'Take care! It is all a trick for they mean to feed you to the bears which lurk in the woods!'

After going through the woods for some time, the hunters came to a large open space hedged about with manzanita bushes.
'Lay your nets here,' Datca told the boys. 'My men and I will go further into the woods and flush the rabbits towards you.'

The brothers set to work, but, suddenly, they heard a hoarse growling close at hand. The bushes rustled and parted and two enormous bears lumbered into the clearing. Immediately the boys changed into their hummingbird form and escaped into the air. The elder brother remembered the yellow-jackets and he shook his quiver over the bears.

The effect of the smoke had worn off. The angry hornets poured out of the quiver towards the bears and began to sting them again and again. The bears yelped and tried to beat off the hornets with their paws. Then, howling in agony, they disappeared into the woods.

When the boys returned to the Sun Village, Datca was convulsed with rage to see that they had once again thwarted his attempts to kill them, and he decided to attack them openly.

As soon as the boys saw the Sun People advancing towards them with their spears and clubs, they once more transformed themselves into birds. The Sun People hurled their spears and shot their arrows, but the Hummingbird brothers, darting and weaving above their heads, managed to dodge the missiles.

Now it was the younger brother's turn to remember the yellow-jackets. He shouted to the Bird People to take cover and shook his upended quiver.

The hornets streamed from the quiver straight towards the Sun People and attacked them fiercely. The Sun People scattered in all directions, seeking to escape the onslaught, but the hornets, infuriated at having been so long confined, pursued them relentlessly and stung every one of them to death.

The Bird People, who had taken refuge in one of the houses, were all unharmed. They filled their baskets with the Sun People's provisions and then, led by the brave Hummingbird brothers, set out for home.

Old Turtle Woman was overjoyed to see again the friends and relations whom she had long since given up for dead. A great feast was prepared and the singing and dancing went on late into the night. The story of the Hummingbird brothers' daring adventure was told and retold around the campfires countless times.

The Bird People remained contentedly on the shores of Clear Lake for many years until the day that Coyote gave them dancing costumes of feathers and changed them into birds forever to travel the world.

The woman and the butterflies

The woman sat cross-legged on the earthen floor of her hut, listlessly pounding acorns. Her husband had left early to go fishing and she felt bored and lonely. Outside the hut, the sun was shining and the village was busy. She could hear the chattering voices of the other women as they went about their daily work in the open air. Some were cooking or drying the meat which the men had brought back from hunting; others were cleaning skins or weaving baskets and nets. But the woman had no inclination to join them for she was weary of their gossip.

Her little son was discontented too. He crawled about her knees and tugged at her willowbark apron, whining for attention. Finally, in exasperation, the woman threw down her pestle and snatched him up. At once the baby laughed and crowed and the woman, in spite of her ill-humour, began to laugh too.

'Ah, my son!' she said. 'You are as restless as I am! Perhaps a change of air will do us both good. Let us go up into the hills where the wind is fresh and the birds sing. After all, I can gather roots and seeds at the same time.'

She strapped the baby on to his cradleboard and slung him on her back. Then she gathered up her digging-stick, her seed-beater and her basket and left the hut. The other women called to her, but she pretended not to hear and walked quickly out of the village.

The sun grew warmer as she climbed into the hills. Now and again she stopped to beat seeds from the slender grasses and collected them in her basket. By mid-day she had left the village far behind and she was hot and out of breath.

She stopped to rest in the shade of a manzanita bush, laying her tools down by her side and slipping the cradleboard from her shoulders. The air was warm and heavy with the scent of flowers, birds sang high overhead and gaily coloured butterflies fluttered all round her. The woman leaned back against the bush, idly watching their giddy flight.

One of the butterflies settled on a branch of the manzanita bush. The baby stretched out his short, plump fingers towards the butterfly, but it fluttered out of his reach. It hovered round his head, brushing his cheek with its soft wings, and the baby, shrieking with laughter, tried again to clutch the bright, flickering insect. The woman smiled to see his delight and quickly tried to trap the butterfly with her seed-beater,

but it bobbed away from her and came to rest on a higher branch.

The woman rose slowly and carefully to her knees and crawled cautiously towards the branch, one hand outstretched to clasp the fragile, quivering wings. Closer and closer she inched, but again the butterfly fluttered away and her fingers closed on empty air. She ran after it, darting this way and that to seize it, but always the butterfly danced just out of reach.

She stopped to draw breath and looked back towards the baby. He was quiet now, dozing in the warm sunshine. He would not miss her for a moment or two if she followed the butterfly a little way. She would catch it for him.

Now the butterfly was very near, clinging to a tall, grass stem. The woman rushed towards it, but yet again it flew off. Somehow, it was no longer a game. The woman desperately wanted to capture the butterfly. It was so beautiful, so much larger and more splendid than all the others, with its dappled wings of scarlet, black and gold. She forgot her sleeping baby under the manzanita bush. She forgot her husband and her home in the village. She had eyes and thoughts only for the shimmering butterfly fluttering before her.

On and on through the long afternoon the woman followed the butterfly. It seemed almost to tease her, now resting on a flower or twig so that she thought her next step would catch it, now floating high in the air above her head. Always it eluded her, luring her further into the hills.

At last, as the sun began to set, she sank exhausted to the ground. Her deerskin cloak was dirty and torn from the rough bushes, her arms and legs scratched by thorns. She did not know where she was, but she was too tired to care. She closed her eyes, but still the bright wings of the butterfly seemed to dance before her.

A gentle touch on her arm awoke her from a restless sleep. She opened her eyes and started up. It was morning and a young man knelt by her side. He wore a breechcloth of yellow buckskin and his long hair was bound with a scarlet band.

He said, 'I am the butterfly which you followed yesterday. Will you follow me always?'

The woman was dazzled by his graceful beauty. 'Yes!' she cried. 'Oh yes, I will!'
'Then we will go on together,' said the Butterfly

Man. 'Another day's travel will bring us to my country and there we will settle down. The way is dangerous, for we must pass through many butterflies who will try to take you from me. You must go where I go, step where I step.'

The woman promised to do as he said and they set off, the Butterfly Man leading and the woman following close behind. After many miles they came to the entrance of a great valley.

The Butterfly Man said, 'Beyond this valley lies my home, but this is the most perilous part of our journey, for we are now entering the Valley of Butterflies. No human being has ever reached the other side alive. You will be safe as long as you keep your eyes to the ground and do not look at any of the butterflies. Hold tightly to my belt and do not let go. If you once loosen your grasp, you will be lost forever and I must go on without you.'

The woman gripped his belt with both hands and fixed her eyes on the ground. As they entered the valley the butterflies clustered around them. The woman felt their gentle wings buffeting her body. They hovered in her face and settled among her hair. Despite the Butterfly Man's warning, she raised her eyes and gasped in wonder. The air was filled with countless butterflies, fluttering and swirling like petals in the wind. There were so many of them and so brilliant! All the colours imaginable glowed in their wings.

One, large and black, and glossy as a raven's feather, flitted close by and impulsively her hand shot out towards it. In an instant it was gone, but there were others, many, many others. With both hands she reached out greedily, wanting them all.

The Butterfly Man did not stop or look back. The woman ran after him, but another butterfly took her attention and then another, and she darted in pursuit of them. She fell further and further behind. The Butterfly Man kept on walking until at last the bright curtain of butterflies hid him from view.

The woman scarcely noticed that he had gone. She was completely obsessed and bewitched by the butterflies. She ran here and there, leaping and spinning, snatching first at one, then at another.

She never caught a single one, but all that day, and for many days afterwards, she continued her hopeless chase in the valley, until, worn out, she died there, alone among the butterflies.

Symbols in the North American Indian myths

At the beginning of each chapter the artist has illustrated some of the objects and symbols identified with the characters and events of the story.

TITLE PAGE Symbols and artifacts from the main tribal groups surround the face of a shaman (or holy man), the storyteller of the tribe. Top: Eskimo with Raven the creator, Amikuk the Sea Serpent and Aziwugum, a dog-like monster covered in scales. From the Northern Forests the great hare (Gluskap, Michabo, Nanabozho or Wisagatcak). From the Eastern Woodlands, masks of the Iroquois False Face Society. From the North-West Coast the bear and its Haida stylised portrait. From the Plains, buffalo and hunter. From the South-West, a Hopi Kachina doll and from the Far West, desert plants and animals which figure in the tribal myths.

p. 10 The map shows the positions of the traditional tribal homelands in the late 18th century. Many of the tribes were nomadic, following game or changing their camps according to season. Some, over a period of many years, moved great distances. Cheyenne legends, for example, suggest that this tribe once lived around the Great Lakes before migrating southwards into the Plains. Several tribes moved because of war with others or with European settlers. Some tribes were assimilated into others or became extinct altogether through warfare and disease. Many, in the 19th century, entered reservations which were sometimes far from their traditional homelands.

p. 11 THE FIRST AMERICANS Objects and designs from the different tribal groups. From the Far North (top) walrus, harpoon and bow. From the North-West Coast a stylized Haida pattern represents Raven. Below this, also from the North-West Coast tribes are salmon and Tlingit fish hook. On either side are patterns from the Plains Indians, with a buffalo hide shield. The hare occurs in many tribal myths, from the Northern Forests and Eastern Woodlands to the Plains and the South-West. In the South-West corn was the most important food crop and formed the basis for a settled, agricultural way of life. The butterfly and hummingbird come from the Far West Pomo and Maidu stories in the book. The Hopi pattern at the bottom of the picture represents an Eagle.

p. 16 THE COMING OF RAVEN An Alaskan Eskimo story explaining the creation of the world by Raven. Here he holds the fragment of mica from which the sun was formed.

p. 21 SEDNA, THE WITCH UNDER THE SEA A central Eskimo story. The sea birds and animals of the story surround Sedna herself. Eskimo hunting equipment (below) included harpoons and hunting knives.

p. 25 THE ORIGIN OF THE WINDS An Alaskan Eskimo story. The picture shows the doll which brought the winds, with the tree from whose wood it was carved. Eskimo dolls such as this were made for girls, (boys were given small bows and arrows and models of sleds and kayaks).

p. 29 THE WOMAN AND THE GIANT An Alaskan Eskimo story. The mountain giant Kinak provides caribou for the woman to eat. Below is the basket in which she collected the ear tips off the animals he gave her. These later turned into complete pelts overnight—an important source of clothing and wealth. Alaskan Eskimo tools (below) included knives for hunting, skinning and cutting up game and fish.

p. 34 HARE AND OTTER A Micmac story. The great Hare with a fishing pole and fish hooks, with, above, barbed fishing spears. The bowl contains cooked eels. Above this is a typical birchbark wigwam and Otter, the victim of the Hare's trickery.

p. 39 THE SEVEN SISTERS An Ojibwa story about the constellation of the Pleiades. The girl's dress (here and in the colour illustration on page 42) is based on paintings by Peter Rindisbacher, a Swiss artist who travelled around the Great Lakes area in the early 19th century.

p. 44 GLUSKAP, LORD OF THE NORTH A Micmac story. Typical Micmac patterns from beadwork designs (used to decorate clothing) surround animals in the story, the fern root which killed Gluskap's brother, a moose whistle used to attract animals for hunting and an arrow. The three birch bark boxes in the centre contain the wishes granted by Gluskap. These boxes were made in the 18th century, but probably not before contact with whites. They were probably learned from and made for Europeans.

p. 48 THE GIRL WHO MARRIED A BEAR A Tsimshian story. The bear was an important crest or totem. At the bottom of the picture is a design representing a bear, probably taken from a pattern appliqued onto a wool blanket. The Tsimshian hunting implements are arrows, club, bow and quiver.

p. 53 RAVEN AND THE BEAVERS A Haida story. The illustration shows elements from the story—Raven with the salmon lake in his beak, salmon and beavers.

p. 58 ONLY ONE, THE GREAT SHAMAN A Tshimshian story. A shaman's bear claw head-dress, drum, dancing apron and ceremonial rattle. The wasp represents the stinging wasps which Only One passed through to his initiation in the cave.

p. 64 THE STRONG MAN A Tlingit story. At the top is a Tlingit canoe, used for walrus hunting. The Strong Man himself carries a carved club, used for killing seals and is surrounded by carved hunting knives and Tlingit patterns from woodcarving designs.

p. 68 THE BIG TURTLE A Huron story. The illustration shows the apple tree which fell from the sky with the swans which carried the sky woman on their backs. The lower panel contains elements from the second Turtle story.

p. 73 THE WAMPUM BIRD An Iroquois story. Wampum beads were used as decorations, also as a form of currency and as records of treaties. The Wampum belt (top) symbolizes friendship. The distinctive ball-headed club was usually carved out of one piece of wood. Below, an Iroquois warrior dressed for hunting.

p. 77 WHY THE OPPOSUM'S TAIL IS BARE A Cherokee story. Cherokee patterns from baskets with the animals of the story, a Cherokee drum and drum stick used in dances and gourd rattle.

p. 81 THE MORNING STAR A Blackfoot story. A Blackfoot warrior ceremonially dressed with lance ornamented with feathers and necklace of beads. His clothes consist of buckskin decorated with coloured glass beads obtained from traders. The plant is the giant turnip. Feather woman (below) is surrounded by Blackfoot patterns from painted rawhide bags.

p. 85 SCAR FACE AND THE SUN DANCE A Blackfoot story. Sundance head-dress (after an engraving in the American Museum of Natural History).

p. 90 BEHIND THE WATERFALL A Cheyenne story, part of a long epic about the hero Sweet Medicine. Here he brings knowledge of growing corn and hunting buffalo to his tribe.

p. 92 THE SEARCH FOR THE BUFFALO A Blackfoot story. A tribal chief in ceremonial feather head-dress and ornaments, with Little Dog and Napi in their disguises. Below the buffalo is a Blackfoot pipe used for ceremonies and solemn occasions, and a buffalo hide shield used in warfare.

p. 97 THE ADVENTURES OF IKTOMI A Sioux story. Iktomi, dressed as a hunter in horned head-dress, with Rabbit, the buffalo skull and mice of the story. Below is a Sioux shield made of buffalo hide and painted with a stylised eagle.

p. 102 HASJELTI'S DANCE A Navajo story. At the top is part of a sand-painting used in a curing ceremony. The figures are representations of the Holy People. Below the crows and the rainbow (symbolizing Nattsilit, the rainbow woman) are the Holy People disguised as sheep. At the bottom is a detail from a Navajo blanket design.

p. 105 After a sandpainting prepared for Hajelti's Dance Ceremonial. To avoid offending religious feeling, one of the leaves has been omitted.

p. 107 THE CORN MAIDENS A Zuni story. Paiyatuma and his flute with ears of corn and a Zuni woman in ceremonial dress, tending the all important corn plant.

p. 112 RABBIT SHOOTS THE SUN A Hopi story, Hopi patterns surround Rabbit shooting his arrows at the sun. Below is a round Hopi basket.

p. 114 THE THEFT OF FIRE A Ute story. Coyote in his reed wig with the birds who helped him carry fire and, below, a campfire.

p. 121 THE HUMMINGBIRD BROTHERS A Pomo story. The illustration shows the brothers as hummingbirds and, below, in human form. The oak leaves and acorns are from the white oak. Acorns were a staple food, stored for use throughout the year.

p. 125 THE WOMAN AND THE BUTTERFLIES A Maidu story. Vast migrations of butterflies such as the Monarch species here may have given rise to this story. The woman is wearing a ceremonial dress. Her ordinary costume would have been a simple skirt of shredded bark. At her feet are a seed beater, digging stick and basket for collecting grass seeds.

The names

In general, Indian names are pronounced just as they look, that is to say phonetically. Until the arrival of Europeans, none of the many languages and dialects were written down and so the spelling of Indian words and names results from the attempts of European explorers and settlers to speak and write the languages of the tribes whom they encountered. However, because these Europeans were of different nationalities, their spelling often varied. The French, for example, might use one spelling, the English another, while later generations might corrupt both. 'Sioux' comes from 'Nadowessioux', the French version of the Ojibwa name for the tribe, 'Nadowessiweg' meaning 'snakes' (and so 'enemies'). In the early 19th century Americans took the last two syllables of the French name and pronounced it 'soo'. Similarly, 'Navajo' is a Spanish name, originally 'Apaches de Nabaju', from the name given to them by their Pueblo neighbours and meaning 'enemies of the cultivated fields'. (The Spanish 'j' is pronounced 'h' and so one sometimes finds 'Navajo' anglicized to 'Navaho'). The names which Europeans gave to the Indians were often quite different from those by which the Indians called themselves. Thus the Sioux call themselves 'Dakota' meaning 'friends' or 'allies', while the Navajo call themselves 'Dineh' meaning 'people'.

Indian personal names could also be confusing, since an individual might have several at different periods of his life or even at the same time. Soon after a child was born, the parents asked someone to name the child. This person, who might be a relative or someone highly respected in the community, usually selected a name connected with a dream or vision he or she might have had. It was believed that the spirit power associated with the visions was thus passed to the child. Later in life people might acquire other names derived from their exploits in hunting or war. These were ceremonial names and, because of their special power, used only rarely. The name by which a person was usually known was often a nickname such as 'Little Bear' perhaps given to a child thought to resemble one at birth, or 'Standing Alone', applied to someone with a reserved and aloof manner.

Index